WHY WON'T THEY LISTEN?

WHY WON'T THEY LISTEN?

THE POWER OF CREATION EVANGELISM

KEN HAM

Master
Books

A Division of New Leaf Publishing Group

First printing: July 2002
Eighth printing: September 2011

Master Books® is a division of the New Leaf Publishing Group, Inc.

ISBN: 978-0-89051-378-1
Library of Congress Catalog Card Number: 2002105381

Unless otherwise noted, all Scripture is from the King James Version of the Bible.

Please consider requesting that a copy of this volume be purchased by your local library system.

Printed in the United States of America.

Please visit our website for other great titles:
www.masterbooks.net

For information regarding author interviews, please contact the publicity department at (870) 438-5288.

DEDICATION

This book is dedicated to all my special friends in the town of Dalby, Queensland, Australia — especially the Jiggens and Munro families who have been such a blessing to my family and our ministry. My first teaching appointment was at Dalby State High School. This is also where I first became actively involved in creation evangelism.

ACKNOWLEDGMENTS

First of all, I would like to thank the many people who, over the years, have encouraged me to put in writing my lectures on creation evangelism. I believe that this publication will not only help Christians be more effective in their witnessing, but will also help many more people realize that ministries like Answers in Genesis are not just involved in a debate about creation versus evolution. The creation ministry is ultimately an evangelistic outreach that defends the authority of the Word of God against secular humanism and proclaims the gospel of Jesus Christ.

Secondly, I would like to specifically thank those whose invaluable help enabled me to complete this publication. My sincere thanks to Geoff Stevens and Mark Looy for editorial advice; to Dave Jolly for his hours of research to provide the footnotes; to artist Dan Lietha for using his God-given talents to draw the illustrations; and to many of the secretarial staff at AiG who carried out various tasks to facilitate this project.

CONTENTS

Foreword 11

1. A Worrisome Trend 15

2. What *Is* the Gospel? 23

3. Communication — It's a Problem 33

4. The Cross — A Stumbling Block! 39

5. The Cross — Foolishness! 49

6. Pioneer Evangelism — Outstanding Success 57

7. From "Jews" — to "Greeks" 63

8. The Evolution Connection 73

9. Beauty and the Curse 93

10. The Seven Cs 111

11. Practical Creation Evangelism 123

12. The Generation Gaps 141

13. "Myth-ing" the Point 147

14. The Victory Chapter! 155

I sat in the audience as Ken Ham, renowned creation lecturer and author, asked a question — "Is America as a nation more Christian or less Christian than it once was?" Without hesitation, a resounding "less Christian" was heard from those present.

Ken went on to say that he receives this same answer whenever he asks this question across America, England, Scotland, Wales, and even countries like his homeland of Australia which has never had as much of a Christian basis.

Ken then paused, the audience waiting in expectation for his next statement. In a serious but forceful tone, Ken went on to say, "Do you realize that America has the greatest number of Christian radio and TV stations in the world, the greatest number of Christian bookshops and Christian resources, the greatest number of churches, Christian colleges, Bible colleges, and seminaries, and sends out 80 percent of the missionaries in the world?"

Ken paused once again as a deathly silence fell across the audience. "Friends," he said, "why is it that the nation that has the greatest Christian influence in the world is becoming less Christian every day? Consider the country of England. Before the last war, somewhere around 40 percent or more of the population attended church. However, today the number is more like 5 percent. What happened to England is what is happening to America. And where England is today spiritually, with hardly any vestige of biblical Christianity left in the culture, America will be tomorrow — and for the same basic reasons."

Ken continued, "Now it is true that many in the Church in America realize there is a problem. They know that for some reason, there is an ever-widening gap between the church and the culture. Many are trying to bridge that gap by watering down the teaching of the Word of God and increasing entertainment programs to make the Church look more like the world. And it is true that as a result, some 'mega' churches are arising, seemingly reaching large numbers of people. However, if one stands back and looks at the big picture, there's no doubt, as you told me earlier, that this culture is becoming less Christian every day. Whatever the Church is doing doesn't seem to be working. There is something fundamentally, in fact, foundationally, wrong."

Everyone was deep in thought. Ken then made this very insightful statement, "I believe the main reason the church is not 'touching' the culture like it used to, is because, by and large, the culture has 'touched' the church. Most of the church has allowed the authority of the Word of God to be undermined beginning in Genesis by compromising with evolutionary ideas and/or millions of years. After years of such compromise, the foundational basis of the culture, the absolute authority of the Word of God, has been replaced with a different foundation — one that makes fallible man the ultimate authority. As a result of this foundational change, which the Church itself helped to bring about, the culture has changed in structure from a Christian one to an increasingly secular one."

Ken then challenged the audience with these words: "If we are going to reach the culture of today with the unchanging saving message of the gospel, we have to adopt a different method by which to present the gospel, one in accord with an understanding of this foundational change. If the Church continues on its present road of ignoring the foundational issues that have changed the culture, it will become increasingly ineffective in 'touching' this culture. The slide into secularism will continue to escalate, and America will become the England of tomorrow."

"Why won't they listen?" is what people in the Church ask of today's culture. In this powerful book for the Church today, Ken Ham not only outlines the foundational reasons as to why evangelism doesn't work today as it used to generations ago, but gives the solution from Scripture as to how Christians can begin to turn the culture around.

The power of creation evangelism is set forth in this book to equip and challenge the church to use God's method of evangelism to reach a culture that, by and large, no longer has a Christian basis.

Ken's heart is to see the gospel proclaimed and lives changed as a result. However, today we need people like those specially mentioned in 1 Chronicles 12:32, "*And of the children of Issachar, which were men that had understanding of the times, to know what Israel ought to do.*"

We need Christians today who understand the times so they'll know what to do. *Why Won't They Listen?* will teach you how to understand the times and what to do as a result. You will never think the same way about evangelism again after reading this challenging and thought-provoking book. I believe its message has the potential to change the face of any nation where God's people have "understanding of the times."

Tim Dudley
President
New Leaf Publishing Group

CHAPTER 1

A WORRISOME TREND

B
ack in 1975, I was teaching biology and general science in the public (government) school system in Australia. At that time, some of the older teachers were complaining that the students weren't as easy to control as they were in years past. These young people didn't seem to have the same respect or show the required courtesy as previous generations had. No one seemed able to put their finger on it — but all agreed that the behavior of the students reflected an overall change that had occurred in the culture.

Some pastors still taught regular religious education classes in public schools. I was a young, inexperienced teacher, but as a Christian, I had a zeal to reach the students with the truth of God's Word. One day, a group of pastors came to me and explained that they were having great difficulty with their religious education program in the school. They were becoming increasingly frustrated because the students didn't behave themselves very well, and most seemed disinterested in what was being taught.

Pondering what they were telling me as they poured out their hearts, I asked them to explain to me the nature of the curriculum they were teaching these students. These pastors explained that they were teaching such things as Paul's missionary journeys, the gospel of Jesus Christ, His death and resurrection, the new heaven and earth, and other New Testament teachings.

Many of the students, however, were openly disrespectful and showed little if any interest in this Bible teaching. What were these pastors to do? They so wanted these young people to believe and understand the Bible and trust the Lord. How were they to reach them? An older, more experienced pastor commented that the students weren't like this in years past. He had noticed this trend for some time now — but it was getting worse. Why was it increasingly difficult to communicate to *this* generation of students?

The pastors asked me if I could shed any light on this dilemma. The more I thought about it, the more it hit me like a lightning bolt. I had noticed that the biology and general science textbooks were permeated by evolutionary philosophy. Evolution (in the "microbe-to-man" sense) was presented as fact. But it wasn't just in science — evolutionary ideas permeated most courses.

I said to these pastors, "Do you know what these students are being taught in most of their classes? They are being told that they're just animals that evolved from some primeval soup millions of years ago. These young people are being indoctrinated to believe that evolution is science. Because they are growing up in a world full of wonderful technology that is an outgrowth of real science, they have a great respect for what is called science. Sadly, they don't realize that evolution is not science. But, because of the way they are being taught, to them the Bible is just an outdated religious book. After all, in astronomy they learn how the solar system formed by itself from a dust cloud over millions of years. In geology, they are taught that the earth is billions of years old, and the fossil record is the history of the evolution of life. In biology, they are shown pictures of 'ape-men,' considered to be their ancestors. In history, primitive man is presented as going through a Stone Age in an onward, upward evolutionary process."

In other words, I explained to the pastors that day after day, in class after class, these students were being indoctrinated against believing what the Bible has to say about our origins. Even if the teachers didn't specifically mention the Bible, the point was that these students were being taught a way of thinking that inoculates them *against* the Bible.

For instance, I vividly recall one of my students blurting out, "Sir, how can you believe the Bible when it tells us we came from Adam and Eve — and we know from science that this is not true?"

I told this story to the pastors and concluded, "Here's the problem. During their school hours, students are being taught more and more that evolution is fact and science has proved the Bible wrong. They don't believe that God created everything. The textbooks tell them that the universe and life arose by chance, random processes. The students know that evolution and its teachings about 'ape-men' contradict the Bible's teaching about Adam and Eve. Increasingly, some teachers are beginning to be vocal about attacking the Bible. Now these same students are coming to

your religious education classes to hear you teach from the Bible. However, many of them don't even believe now that you can trust the Bible. They don't have a respect for the Bible's teachings. They think that in this scientific age, the Bible is an outdated book. So why should they be interested in listening to what you have to say?"

The pastors had not thought about it in this way before. It made sense. So what were they to do? I suggested that before they could really teach about things like Paul's missionary journeys, or the life of Jesus, and the power of the gospel, they really needed to get the students' attention that the Bible really could be trusted, and it really is the infallible Word of God.

I suggested that they develop a series of lessons to counteract the anti-Christian teaching the students were receiving each day at school. We would look at the textbooks, and then take this erroneous material and critique it — but at the same time show that what the Bible states explained the evidence correctly.

To me, it was vital that the pastors defend the Book of Genesis to the students. After all, if the first book in the Bible can't be trusted in their eyes, why should any other? As one lady put it to me 20 years later, "When my church told me that I had to accept evolution, and that Genesis couldn't be believed as written, I asked, 'When does God start telling the truth then?' "

I had enough interaction with the students to know that this was how their thinking went as well. If in their religious education classes they were being told to believe the New Testament — but they knew from science that the first book in the Bible wasn't true. Why should they trust any of it?

Working with the pastors, we devised a series of lessons that showed the students that evolution was just a belief — there weren't any "ape-men," evolutionists had not proved the earth was billions of years old, there were major problems with their theories about the origin of the solar system, and so on.

When the pastors presented these lessons, they were astonished. The students sat up and listened. They were extremely interested — and they had *lots* of questions. "What about carbon dating then? Where do dinosaurs fit in? Why don't our teachers tell us this information?"

Once the pastors had clearly illustrated that real science had not disproved the Bible and that the Bible can be used to explain the world around us, what a difference it made! Many of the students showed intense interest in spiritual things. Later on, when the pastors began teaching about Jesus in the New Testament, they had much more success in getting these young people to listen and take note.

At the time, I didn't realize that I was involved in developing a method of evangelism that later came to be called "creation evangelism." Not only is this method of evangelism based on the Bible, but it is one of the most powerful methods for reaching today's world with the gospel of Jesus Christ.

This incident with the pastors and the school students came to mind when I went to Japan to speak across the country. The first meeting scheduled was one in which I had the pleasure of meeting with my Japanese translator, Nathan, a man who was born in Japan and who grew up in the culture, and who was the son of an American missionary.

I met his father at one of the meetings. He told me that he and his wife realized that as American missionaries they wouldn't be able to effectively communicate to the Japanese culture. Therefore, they determined that the son they had in Japan was to be their gift to the Japanese people. "We gave our son to Japan," they told me.

Because Nathan grew up in the Japanese culture, not only could he speak their language flawlessly, but he understood the thinking of the Japanese people. In fact, he makes his living as a translator.

The first thing Nathan explained to me was that whenever I used the word "God" he could not just translate this as "God." Because of the prevalence of the Shinto religion in this country, and thus their belief in many gods, the people would just add this "God" I was talking about to all their other gods.

So, whenever I used the word "God," Nathan would define who this God is — the God who created and upholds all things. He is the God who is separate from His creation.

Nathan then went on to relate something else that I had not thought about. Up until the last world war, Christians were persecuted and even killed in Japan. The Japanese culture had no Christian basis whatsoever. In a population of over 150 million people, less than 0.1 percent are considered to be born-again Christians.

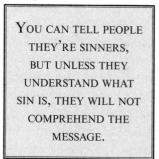

YOU CAN TELL PEOPLE THEY'RE SINNERS, BUT UNLESS THEY UNDERSTAND WHAT SIN IS, THEY WILL NOT COMPREHEND THE MESSAGE.

If I were to tell the average Japanese person that they were sinners and needed to trust in what Christ did on the Cross for them, they wouldn't have any idea what I was talking about.

Without the foundational basis of the account of the Fall in Genesis, and the fact that we all are traced back to one man,

Adam, whom God created, how would they understand the gospel? You can tell people they're sinners, but unless they understand what sin is, they will not comprehend the message.

Nathan explained to me that if I was to communicate the message of the gospel to the average Japanese, I would first need to lay the foundation of the gospel from Genesis, before they would really have much understanding.

He then said that atheistic evolution is taught as fact through the education system in Japan. Probably everyone in Japan had heard of evolution — but not many heard that the Bible can be trusted. Thus, he explained, evolution is considered to be fact, because it is the supposed scientific view of origins. From a human perspective, evolution would have to be counteracted before people would even be willing to listen to the Bible's account of origins on which the plan of salvation is actually based.

And then there is one more problem. Because of the education system and the influence of compromising missionaries from countries like America, many of the Christians in the small conservative churches in Japan believed in evolution, or various aspects of evolutionary philosophy. They themselves did not understand the foundational importance of a literal Adam and a literal Fall. Could this be part of the reason why the Church in Japan was not successful in reaching the culture at large? For this and other reasons (costs, for example), missionaries have been pulling out of Japan. Some now call it a "missionary graveyard."

Much of the Church throughout the world is missing out on using what I know to be one of the most successful means of reaching people with the gospel of Jesus Christ. This technique is useful, even in cultures that have become increasingly devoid of the knowledge of God and His Word — or cultures that have no Christian basis whatsoever.

It's called "creation evangelism."

This is a highly successful method of evangelism that could change entire nations, if only the Church understood it and used it in today's skeptical world.

There's no doubt that our once-Christianized Western nations are not only becoming more secularized, but that an anti-Christian element is growing with increasing fervor. Other nations that have never had a major Christian influence seem so closed to the gospel. How can we reach all these people with the saving message of Jesus Christ?

There is an answer — a powerful answer!

Several years ago, your ministry played an important role in bringing me to the God and Savior of the Bible. If I was going to believe in God, I first had to acknowledge His existence. And if I was going to believe in the God of the Bible, it had to be proven to me that the Scriptures were not in error. Your material addressed the evolution vs. creation [issue] and proved to me the literal truth of the Word.

V.B., New York

CHAPTER 2

WHAT *IS* THE GOSPEL?

S urely the answer to this question is obvious to the average
Christian. The word "gospel" means "good news." When
Christians talk about the gospel, they are presenting the
good news of Christ's death and resurrection. As Paul states in
1 Corinthians 15:1–4:

> Moreover, brethren, *I declare unto you the gospel*
> which I preached unto you, which also ye have received,
> and wherein ye stand; By which also ye are saved, if
> ye keep in memory what I preached unto you, unless
> ye have believed in vain. For I delivered unto you first
> of all that which I also received, *how that Christ died*
> *for our sins according to the scriptures; And that he was*
> *buried, and that he rose again the third day according*
> *to the scriptures* (emphasis added).

Paul doesn't end his explanation of the gospel here. Note
very carefully how Paul explains the gospel message later in this
same passage:

> Now if Christ be preached that he rose from the
> dead, how say some among you that there is no res-
> urrection of the dead? But if there be no resurrection
> of the dead, then is Christ not risen: And if Christ be

not risen, then is our preaching vain, and your faith is also vain. Yea, and we are found false witnesses of God; because we have testified of God that he raised up Christ: whom he raised not up, if so be that the dead rise not.

For if the dead rise not, then is not Christ raised: And if Christ be not raised, your faith is vain; ye are yet in your sins. Then they also which are fallen asleep in Christ are perished. If in this life only we have hope in Christ, we are of all men most miserable. But now is Christ risen from the dead, and become the firstfruits of them that slept. *For since by man came death, by man came also the resurrection of the dead. For as in Adam all die, even so in Christ shall all be made alive. . . . And so it is written, The first man Adam was made a living soul; the last Adam was made a quickening spirit* (1 Cor. 15:12–45, emphasis added).

Notice that in explaining why Jesus died, Paul went to the Book of Genesis and its account of Adam and the Fall. In other words, one cannot really understand *the good news* in the New Testament of Jesus' death and resurrection, and thus payment for sin, until one understands the *bad news* in Genesis of the fall of man, and thus the origin of sin and its penalty of death.

I'll never forget the phone call I received from a pastor's

wife. It went something like this: "Our church can't come to your seminar," she said to me.

"Why not?" I replied.

"Well, you insist on taking Genesis as literal history. But Genesis is not that important —

it's not that essential what one believes about Genesis. Why can't we just agree on the essentials of Christianity?"

"So what do you mean by the essentials?" I asked.

She answered, "The fact that we're all sinners and that Jesus Christ died for our sin. This is what is essential to Christianity. Believing in a literal Genesis is certainly not essential." She then went on and asked me, "If someone is born again as the Bible defines, but doesn't believe in a literal Genesis as you do, is he saved and going to heaven?"

"Well," I replied, "if he is truly born again, even if he doesn't believe in a literal Genesis, of course he is saved and going to heaven."

"See," she blurted out, "Genesis is not essential—what Jesus Christ did on the cross is what is essential to Christianity."

I then asked: "Do you mind if I ask you a question?"

"Go ahead," she responded.

"Why did Jesus die on the Cross?"

She immediately answered, "For our sin."

"And, what do you mean by sin?" I inquired.

"Rebellion," came the answer.

I then asked, "Could you please tell me how you came to define sin as rebellion? Is that your idea or someone else's idea? I've even heard some people define sin as 'a lack of self-esteem.' On what basis have you determined sin means rebellion? Where did you get that definition?"

And her response? "I know what you're trying to do!" she declared. She realized that I had her boxed in. She didn't want to admit that without Genesis, she could not answer the question. Because the meaning of anything (like sin) is dependent on its origin, you could not define sin without referring to the literal event of the Fall in Genesis. The literal rebellion of Adam, as recorded in Genesis, is the foundation necessary to understanding the meaning of sin.

What was I trying to do? Simply this: to demonstrate that the only way we can define sin as rebellion is if there was a literal rebellion. The reason we are all sinners is because, as Paul clearly states, we are all descendants of the first man, Adam. Because there was a literal first Adam, who was in a literal garden, with a literal tree, and took a literal fruit when tempted by a literal serpent, thus there was a literal Fall, which was a literal rebellion.

As Christians, we need to answer this question: Is it essential to believe in a literal Fall? Absolutely! If there was no literal Fall, then what is sin? Who defines it? What then is Paul talking about in 1 Corinthians 15, or even Romans 5:12 where he states, "Wherefore,

Jesus Christ "The Last Adam"
1 Cor. 15:45

For as in Adam all die, even so in Christ shall all be made alive.
1 Cor. 15:22

"The First Adam"
1 Cor. 15:45

Which Adam is "non-essential" to the Gospel?

as by one man sin entered into the world, and death by sin; and so death passed upon all men, for that all have sinned"?

So, in explaining the gospel, Paul discusses the foundations of the gospel in Genesis and the bad news: the origin of sin and its penalty of death. He then tells us the good news of salvation in Christ. In Colossians, in explaining the gospel, Paul also points out clearly that our Savior, the Lord Jesus Christ, is the Creator:

> Who hath delivered us from the power of darkness, and hath translated us into the kingdom of his dear Son: In whom we have redemption through his blood, even the forgiveness of sins: Who is the image of the invisible God, the firstborn of every creature: *For by him were all things created*, that are in heaven, and that are in earth, visible and invisible, whether they be thrones, or dominions, or principalities, or powers: all things were created by him, and for him: And he is before all things, and by him all things consist (Col. 1:13–17, emphasis added).

And so, in Revelation we are told concerning Jesus Christ:

> Thou art worthy, O Lord, to receive glory and honour and power: *for thou hast created* all things, and for thy pleasure they are and were created (Rev. 4:11, emphasis added).

> And they sung a new song, saying, Thou art worthy to take the book, and to open the seals thereof: *for thou wast slain*, and hast redeemed us to God by thy blood out of every kindred, and tongue, and people, and nation (Rev. 5:9, emphasis added).

Our Creator became our Redeemer! The reason this was necessary is because all humans are sinners. Therefore, a sinful person could not die for sin. We needed a perfect man to die for sin. The only solution was for the perfect, sinless Creator to become a man so He could be our Savior! Thus, the doctrine of creation is vital to an understanding of the gospel.

But Paul also goes on to write about the consummation of all things — the final victory that will overcome the effects of the Fall:

> Howbeit that was not first which is spiritual, but that which is natural; and afterward that which is spiritual. The first man is of the earth, earthy: the second man is the Lord from heaven. As is the earthy, such are they also that are earthy: and as is the heavenly, such are they also that are heavenly. And as we have borne the image of the earthy, we shall also bear the image of the heavenly.
>
> Now this I say, brethren, that flesh and blood cannot inherit the kingdom of God; neither doth corruption inherit incorruption. Behold, I shew you a mystery; We shall not all sleep, but we shall all be changed, *In a moment, in the twinkling of an eye, at the last trump: for the trumpet shall sound, and the dead shall be raised incorruptible, and we shall be changed. For this corruptible must put on incorruption, and this mortal must put on immortality. So when this corruptible shall have put on incorruption, and this mortal shall have put on immortality, then shall be brought to pass the saying that is written, Death is swallowed up in victory. O death, where is thy sting? O grave, where is thy victory? The sting of death is sin; and the strength of sin is the law. But thanks be to God, which giveth us the victory through our Lord Jesus Christ* (1 Cor. 15:46–57, emphasis added).

We are given more details of the consummation in 2 Peter 3 and Revelation chapters 21 and 22. We're told there will be a new heaven and earth. There will be no more crying, no more death, and the curse (that was imposed because of sin as we read in Genesis 3) will be no more:

> And God shall wipe away all tears from their eyes; *and there shall be no more death*, neither sorrow, nor crying, neither shall there be any more pain: for the former things are passed away (Rev. 21:4, emphasis added).

And there shall *be no more curse* (Rev. 22:3, emphasis added).

Nevertheless we, according to his promise, look for new heavens and a new earth, wherein dwelleth righteousness (2 Pet. 3:13).

With all this as background, I now want to explain that an understanding of the following three elements of the gospel is a prerequisite to an understanding of how to present the gospel to different people within a culture, or to different cultures. Consider this:

1. If one preaches the gospel without the message of the Creator, and the origin of sin and death, then one preaches it without the foundational knowledge that is necessary to understand the rest of the gospel. Without this information, who then is Jesus Christ? Why did He need to die? Why could He, and not someone else, die for sin? What is special about Christ? Where did sin come from? Why can we say that all have sinned? Why do we die?

2. If one preaches a gospel without the message of Christ crucified and raised from the dead, then one preaches a gospel without power. After all, as Paul said, *"And if Christ be not raised, your faith is vain; ye are yet in your sins"* (1 Cor. 15:17). The only reason our personal sins can be forgiven and our relationship with our Creator be restored is because of what Christ did on the cross. The death and resurrection of Jesus Christ is central to the gospel. That's why the message of the "Jesus Seminar" movement is so destructive. A leading scholar in this group, Marcus Borg, denies the Virgin Birth, the Resurrection, and many other non-negotiables of the Christian faith. He identifies himself as a Christian, and is received in many churches, yet according to Scripture, his faith is in vain. Interestingly, Borg often begins his lectures by trying to assign Genesis to the realm of myth.

> **WE NEED TO UNDERSTAND THAT DEATH IS AN INTRUSION IN OUR WORLD.**

3. A gospel that is preached without the message of the new heaven and earth is a message preached without hope. What point is there to a gospel with no future sinless state? Because of sin and the judgment of the curse, the creation is "groaning" (Rom. 8:22). There is death, sickness, and suffering all around us. However, we need to understand that death is an intrusion in our world.

In 1 Corinthians 15:26, Paul states it this way: "The last *enemy* that shall be destroyed is death" (emphasis added).

Death, then, is an enemy that is to be destroyed some time in the future. Peter informs us that we are to look forward to this future time: "Nevertheless we, according to his promise, look for new heavens and a new earth, wherein dwelleth righteousness" (2 Pet. 3:13).

And we are given a glimpse of what this future state will be like in the Book of Revelation:

> And I saw a new heaven and a new earth: for the first heaven and the first earth were passed away; and there was no more sea (Rev. 21:1).

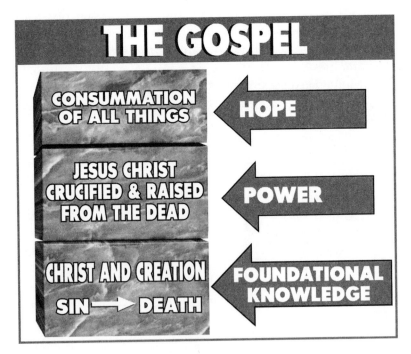

> And God shall wipe away all tears from their eyes; and there shall be no more death, neither sorrow, nor crying, neither shall there be any more pain: for the former things are passed away (Rev. 21:4).

> And there shall be no more curse (Rev. 22:3).

What a time to look forward to, when we will be free from death, pain, sickness, and suffering! As my colleague and friend Dr. Gary Parker says, "The only time we actually receive *complete* healing is when we die."

In essence, the three elements in the illustration are necessary to fully comprehend the gospel and thus the ultimate meaning of Christianity.

Now, recall our discussion in the first chapter. The students weren't interested in the power of the gospel, or the new heaven and earth, because they had in reality been taught that the foundation of the gospel (that God created all things and there was a first man Adam, who rebelled, and thus we are all sinners condemned to death) was *false*.

Now, these students were in the school system in the 1970s. As we begin our new millennium, the textbooks are even more blatantly anti-Christian. Evolution is presented as fact. By and large, students are told they are just animals, there is no purpose and meaning in life, science has proved that God is not necessary to explain the universe and life, and so on. For them, the pain, death, and suffering that we are reminded of daily are necessary parts of life, and thus are essential to furthering life on this planet (as evolutionary belief teaches). Therefore, how can there be a loving God? Young people are hurting, but they don't understand the real reason why this is so.

Young people today have little or no understanding of what is meant by sin or of its consequences (remember: death and suffering are intrusions — results of sin). They are growing up in a culture that teaches them they are just evolved animals and that there is no Creator God to whom they are accountable. Logically, then, there is no basis for absolutes (which of course is their absolute!). Everyone has a right to his or her own opinion.

There must be a tolerance of all views (although Christianity is considered intolerant, because it is exclusive — Jesus Christ is the only way). For them "truth" is relative. Television programs and movies portray accepted "norms" as sex outside marriage, gratuitous violence, materialism, and sensual pleasure. Human life is not really considered special.

If students back in the 1970s were losing the foundational knowledge to listen or even understand the gospel of Jesus Christ, how much more today has this problem been compounded in Western nations by an increasingly secular education system, media, and society in general?

And in countries like Japan, where there is no Christian basis, how could they ever understand the gospel without the foundational knowledge of the Creator, sin, and thus the need for salvation?

Understanding the foundational aspects of the gospel in Genesis is a vital *key* to unlock a powerful method of evangelism to reach the world for Christ.

I was already a Christian, albeit a young one, and creation had played a part in my conversion, but I realize now that I had only scratched the surface. The way you connected it to the rest of the Bible and to society was brilliant — you made me realize how little I had really understood about sin and death.

I was like the lady you quote in your talks who said, "Being a Christian was like starting to watch a film (or movie) from halfway through. You showed me the beginning; now I understand the plot."

I want to thank you for kick-starting my Christian life, and for helping me to understand the rest of the Bible in a way only an understanding of, and a belief in, a literal Genesis, can achieve, particularly for those of us who did not have a godly upbringing.

G.D., United Kingdom

CHAPTER 3

COMMUNICATION — IT'S A PROBLEM

There are many reasons why the gospel spread so remarkably in the first century. However, I personally believe most Christians, including most Christian leaders, evangelists, and Bible teachers, have not really considered the methodology employed by the early Christians when they encountered their new audiences.

The Book of Acts is given its name because it contains the acts of the apostles in carrying out the Great Commission. Here we have examples for preachers, teachers, and missionaries so that they can carry out the task of presenting the gospel.

One thing that is often missed concerning these early Christians is that they started preaching and witnessing to their audience, *beginning at the level of understanding these people had in relation to Christian beliefs.* In other words, they had to start with a common denominator — there had to be communication at a common level that was understood. Thus, starting at the level that corresponded to the background of a particular culture, the missionaries went on from there to direct their hearts and minds to Christ.

I believe that our method of communication often lies at the heart of some of the difficulties we have in evangelizing in today's world. Let me give you an analogy.

A missionary once explained to me that even though he had gone to a university and learned the language of a particular culture, when he went to live in that culture and preach the Word of God, he had great difficulty in communication.

For instance, he told me about a time he was speaking to a tribe of dark-skinned people in Irian Jaya (north of Australia). He told them that the blood of Jesus would cleanse away the dark spots of sin and make them pure and white and clean before the Lord. But the people he was speaking to were perplexed. They wanted to know why the blood of Jesus made a person dirty. He had run into a problem of communication. It took quite a while, but eventually he figured out the problem.

Because these were a dark-skinned culture, they understood what the missionary had said in a totally different way. When the white ash from their fire was on their skin — they were dirty, but also white! Thus, when the missionary said that Jesus' blood made their souls white, they understood that this meant that Jesus' blood made them dirty!

This missionary told me that if anyone thinks that just because they have learned a different language that they will be able to communicate to a different culture, they need to think again! One can have a great grasp of the language, but may still not communicate, unless there is an understanding of the culture and how the language is used within the culture.

Missionaries abound with similar stories. Many of us smile as these accounts are related. But sadly, most Christians don't realize the importance of the underlying message that these intriguing true-life adventures have for all of us in communicating the gospel.

It also ought to be said at this stage that even if people speak the same language but come from different cultures, then the same words or phrases can have very different meanings. Because I am an Australian who has lived in America for many years, I can give many examples to illustrate this.

I recall many years ago when we still lived in Australia, but I had conducted a number of speaking tours in America. A teenage girl from America came to visit us at our home in Brisbane.

Our son Jeremy was just a baby. I was trying very hard to be nice and hospitable toward this American teenager. So I asked her if she would like to nurse our baby.

From the horrified look on her face, anyone would have thought I had highly insulted her or said something terrible. She was at a loss for words to respond. Without thinking, I told her that it didn't matter, and that I would just continue to nurse the baby. Again she reacted in shock. I couldn't even begin to describe the look on her face.

At this stage, I realized there must be some great gap in our communication. Suddenly, I remembered something from my previous visits to the United States. And then I understood what had happened.

In Australia, "nursing the baby" just means to hold (or cuddle) a baby. In America, "nursing a baby" means to breast-feed a baby. I remember saying to myself, *I just asked this girl to breast-feed our baby! If that wasn't bad enough, I said I would do it!* I wondered whether this girl must have thought that we Australian males had gone through some onward, upward, evolutionary mutational change, so now we could nurse our babies!

You see, the same words from the same language, but used in different cultures, had totally different meanings!

After I had related this story at a seminar in America, one lady asked me, "Well, what do Australians call it when you breast-feed a baby?"

And my reply? "Well, we call it breast-feeding a baby. After all, that's what you do, isn't it?" And that's another aspect of Australian culture people need to understand. The average Australian is rather blunt and just tells it "like it is." (This has actually caused me to get into trouble many times in America.)

Having now lived in America for many years, I think I could write a whole book just on the problems of an Australian communicating in such a culture. There are many differences. But let's consider a totally different culture.

Carl, a close friend of mine who is American by birth, is married to a Japanese national. One day Carl and I were sharing jokes with each other in front of his wife. We thought these jokes

35

were hilarious. However, Carl's wife didn't laugh at one of them. She then said to us, "I don't see what's funny." So we tried to explain the jokes in detail. She then stated, "The Japanese people don't think like that. We don't understand why you would think they are funny."

As I have traveled around other parts of the world, mixing with different cultures, I have increasingly come to realize how important it is to understand how people think, *before* trying to communicate with them.

Time and time again, I've had missionaries tell me, "You shouldn't say that in this culture, it means something totally different." Or, "They didn't understand that particular point, because they don't think like this."

I can smile now, but I was highly embarrassed when my Japanese translator said to me after I had finished my speaking tour in Japan: "Remember how the Japanese people laughed heartily at some of your jokes?"

"Yes," I replied.

"Well, I have to tell you that I knew they wouldn't understand your joke at all. They just don't think like that. I told them that Mr. Ham just told a joke, so please be polite and laugh."

But there is another problem in communication that most Christians are unaware of. Even within the *same* culture, there can be massive communication gaps. People often talk about the "generation gap." I suggest there is an increasing generation gap in our Western cultures. This will become much clearer later in this book. It will suffice for now to say that the more we have generations of unchurched people in an increasingly secularized culture, the more those who are churched will not be able to effectively communicate to them. In essence, it's like communicating with a different culture — the same words either have different meanings or are even meaningless.

For example, many Christian denominations use phrases and jargon that have no relevance for younger generations. Sermons and even hymns can point to "being washed in the blood," or "crossing over Jordan," and increasingly large numbers of people will have no idea what those things mean. It's almost as if traditional Christianity is now just another sub-culture, complete with its own terminology.

In the next two chapters, we are going to look at two particular sermons in the Book of Acts that may bring some surprises for many Christians. We will see that when these sermons are examined in the light of our discussion above, they give us clear examples of not only how to preach the gospel in different cultures, but how to reach an increasingly anti-God Western culture (and other nations).

Two years ago, both my best friend and myself became believers in our Lord Jesus after watching the video set by Ken Ham and Gary Parker called *Understanding Genesis.* At the time, we were quite shocked because when we watched them, we never expected to become converted. We had both read the Bible out of what we thought was political and historical interest, but until we saw the video material, we thought that it was not possible for the Bible to be true because of science.

We have spent most of our time since studying the Bible, searching the Scriptures daily for protection against all the strange teaching that seems to be in churches. We are grateful to your ministry for its emphasis on sound doctrine starting at the beginning at the Book of Genesis, and establishing a proper foundation.

T.H., United Kingdom

CHAPTER 4

THE CROSS
— A STUMBLING BLOCK!

P lease keep the following verse in the back of your mind as we begin our study of two sermons in the Book of Acts (Acts 2 and Acts 17).

> But we preach Christ crucified, unto the Jews a stumbling block, and unto the Greeks foolishness (1 Cor. 1:23).

In this section, we are going to look in detail at the meaning of the first part of the phrase, "unto the Jews a stumbling block."

A tremendous example of successful evangelism in the first century is what happened on the Day of Pentecost, as recorded in Acts 2.

> Ye men of Israel, hear these words; *Jesus of Nazareth, a man approved of God among you by miracles and wonders and signs, which God did by him in the midst of you, as ye yourselves also know: Him*, being delivered by the determinate counsel

and foreknowledge of God, *ye have taken, and by wicked hands have crucified and slain*: Whom God hath raised up, having loosed the pains of death: because it was not possible that he should be holden of it.

For David speaketh concerning him, I foresaw the Lord always before my face, for he is on my right hand, that I should not be moved: Therefore did my heart rejoice, and my tongue was glad; moreover also my flesh shall rest in hope: Because thou wilt not leave my soul in hell, neither wilt thou suffer thine Holy One to see corruption. Thou hast made known to me the ways of life; thou shalt make me full of joy with thy countenance.

Men and brethren, let me freely speak unto you of *the patriarch David*, that he is both dead and buried, and his sepulchre is with us unto this day. Therefore being a prophet, and knowing that God had sworn with an oath to him, that of the fruit of his loins, according to the flesh, he would raise up Christ to sit on his throne; He seeing this *before spake of the resurrection of Christ*, that his soul was not left in hell, neither his flesh did see corruption. *This Jesus hath God raised up, whereof we all are witnesses.*

Therefore being by the right hand of God exalted, and having received of the Father the promise of the Holy Ghost, he hath shed forth this, which ye now see and hear. For David is not ascended into the heavens: but he saith himself, The LORD said unto my Lord, Sit thou on my right hand, Until I make thy foes thy footstool. Therefore let all the house of Israel know assuredly, *that God hath made that same Jesus, whom ye have crucified, both Lord and Christ.*

Now when they heard this, *they were pricked in their heart, and said unto Peter and to the rest of the apostles, Men and brethren, what shall we do?* Then Peter said unto them, *Repent, and be baptized every one of you in the name of Jesus Christ for the remission of sins*, and ye shall receive the gift of the Holy Ghost. For the promise is unto you, and to your children, and to all that are afar off, even as many as the Lord our God shall call. And with many other words did he testify and exhort, saying, Save yourselves from this untoward generation. Then they that gladly received his word were baptized: *and the same day there were added unto them about three thousand souls* (Acts 2:22–41, emphasis added).

I have had seminary and Bible college students tell me that their professors told them that they should pattern their method of evangelism after Peter's sermon here in Acts 2. In fact, most modern evangelism in a sense is based on this approach. We read that Peter boldly preached the message of the Cross and the Resurrection, and commanded people to repent. Thousands were saved. What a phenomenal rally this was in the history of Christendom!

Actually, this account in Acts does remind us of some of the great crusades of past generations. There's no doubt that there were times when multitudes of people heard some famous evangelist or Bible teacher preach the message of the Cross — and thousands were converted. We can think back to the days of Whitefield, Wesley, Moody, and others.

But let's look at this sermon from Acts 2 in more detail.

First of all, we need to carefully consider to whom this sermon was preached. Following on from our last chapter on communication, we need to understand the background of the people who heard this message. We need to be asking ourselves the question, "Why was Peter so successful in communicating the message of salvation to this group?"

There were really three groups of people in attendance at Peter's sermon:

1. The Jews who lived in Jerusalem and its surrounding area.

2. Jews of the dispersion who had come to Jerusalem from other parts of the world because of the Feast of Pentecost. This is why Acts 1:8 states that

the apostles were to preach in Jerusalem first, and then spread out.

3. Jewish proselytes who were not Jews by race, but Gentiles who had been converted to the Jewish religion.

THERE IS NO DOUBT THAT THE PEOPLE PETER PREACHED TO *ALREADY HAD THE FOUNDATIONAL KNOWLEDGE OF THE GOSPEL.*

Now, even though there were three different groups of people, they all had one thing in common. They all had an Old Testament background. Let's consider some of the doctrines they would have all understood from the Scriptures:

1. They believed in the one true Creator God.

2. They understood God was the lawgiver and that there were absolutes. Therefore, they *knew* what was right and what was wrong.

3. There was an understanding of Adam's fall and thus that all humans (being his descendants) were sinners under judgment by their Creator.

4. It was understood that the penalty for sin was death. They knew of the thousands of animals that had been sacrificed in their history because of sin. Actually, they were in Jerusalem to sacrifice animals for the same reason.

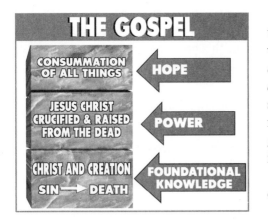

We could say that the culture Peter was speaking to was *a creation-based (Genesis) culture.* Consider again the three main parts of the gospel we discussed in chapter 2.

There is no doubt that the people

Peter preached to *already had the foundational knowledge of the gospel.* They believed in the Creator God and understood sin and its penalty of death. Yet these people, by and large, did not believe that Jesus Christ was the Messiah.

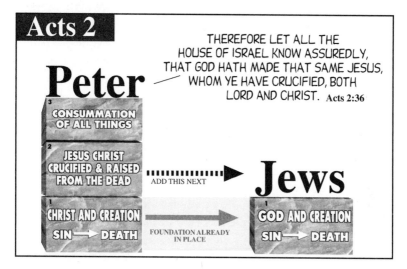

Peter didn't have to convince them concerning the truth of creation. He didn't have to convince Jews that there was such a thing as sin. He didn't have to convince them that the Holy Scripture was God's infallible Word. The problem they had was not accepting that Jesus Christ was God manifest in the flesh and was the Messiah. This was their stumbling block.

From a human perspective, Peter, therefore, had to convince the Jews that Jesus was the Messiah, and that His death and resurrection were vital to their salvation. It was only by accepting what Christ did on the cross that they could have their sins forgiven.

Let me digress for a moment. In this and the next chapter, I will discuss how Peter needed to convince the Jews of some point, or Paul needed to convince the Greek philosophers concerning biblical truths. However, even though these men would do all they could to convince their hearers of truth, from God's perspective we know that He is really the One who opens their heart so that they will listen and understand.

For instance, concerning Paul's preaching, we read words like: *reasoned, disputing* and *persuading* (Acts 17:2; 18:4,19; 19:8–9; 24:25); *proving* and *alleging* (Acts 9:22; Acts 17:3); *disputed* (Acts 9:29); and *mightily convinced* (Acts 18:28).

Paul used every argument he could to convince his hearers of God's Word, knowing that ultimately, of course, it wasn't Paul who did the convincing. Nonetheless, as God's Word states in Isaiah 1:18: "Come now, and let us reason together, saith the Lord."

This is why in 1 Peter 3:15, Christians are commanded to: "Sanctify the Lord God in your hearts: and be ready always to give an answer to every man that asketh you a reason of the hope that is in you with meekness and fear."

From a human perspective, we need to diligently attempt to convince people of the truth of God's Word, using reasoned arguments and explanations that make sense to the hearer.

Over and over again, the prophets, apostles, and Jesus Christ himself called upon people to come to God in repentance. The word "repentance" literally means "to change one's mind." At the same time, the Scripture plainly states, "As it is written, There is none righteous, no, not one: There is none that understandeth, there is none that seeketh after God" (Rom. 3:10–11).

And in Ephesians 2:1 we read, "And you hath he quickened, who were dead in trespasses and sins."

The word "dead" in this passage is the same word used when Lazarus (John 11) is described as being dead. Dead persons can't do anything on their own. Therefore, of ourselves, we can't do anything to come to Christ.

But Romans 10:9 states, "That if thou shalt confess with thy mouth the Lord Jesus, and shalt believe in thine heart that God hath raised him from the dead, thou shalt be saved."

There are, of course, many other passages that we could examine. Personally, I don't think any of us will ever fully understand the above paradox. We are sinful finite beings, trying to understand the mind of the infinite Creator.

We do know that we are commanded to preach (Rom. 10) and that "it pleased God by the foolishness of preaching to save them that believe" (1 Cor. 1:21).

To summarize: The Bible makes it clear that human argument alone is definitely insufficient to bring unbelievers to a knowledge of the truth. One could say that apart from the intervention of God's Holy Spirit, people are not just waiting until the first Christian comes along with an explanation of the gospel, telling them that it's true, so then they'll believe.

I once heard someone say that "faith is not created by reasoning — but neither is it created without it."

All of this discussion brings up another important point. We can't just take clumps of Scripture that we have learned and throw these out hoping that people will respond. We need to heed the lessons from the prophets, apostles, and Jesus — God's Word and the meaning of the gospel must be carefully explained and "argued." And this must be done in such a way that the people hearing the message will understand. Jesus certainly made frequent use of illustrations people were familiar with from nature and agriculture to help them comprehend vital truths.

It is true that God's Word will not return unto Him "void" (Isa. 55:11) — but at the same time, we must present God's Word the way God indicates in Scripture. Human responsibility and God's sovereignty go hand in hand.

Now in returning to the situation with Peter on the Day of Pentecost, we could say that Peter didn't need to deal much with the foundations of the gospel message. He could assume that the foundational knowledge of creation, sin, and death was understood and accepted by his hearers. He could also assume that when he used the word "sin," his audience would have the same understanding as he did. They had the same law, and believed in the same lawgiver. They knew the Ten Commandments. Thus, in their minds, they all understood that

adultery, murder, stealing, and idolatry were sin.

That is why Peter's generation was so readily "pricked in their heart" (Acts 2:37). They *already knew* they were sinners in rebellion against God's law. Peter went on to explain that now they needed to understand that Jesus Christ was their Creator and lawgiver. He was the Messiah. It was His death on the cross that paid the penalty for their sin.

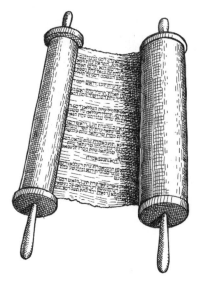

Also, notice that Peter used familiar Scriptures as part of his argument. In Acts 2:25–28 he quoted from David (Ps. 16:8–11) regarding his prophecy concerning the Messiah. Earlier in Acts 2 he quoted from Joel 2:28–32 in relation to the Day of Pentecost. Peter spoke to them beginning where they were in their own thinking. He knew what they accepted and understood, and their respect for the Scriptures. In his preaching, he was able to get directly to the main issue concerning their salvation.

The following analogy helps us in summing up Peter's approach.

I have noticed in the rapidly growing subdivision where we live, the builder of a new home takes quite a long time preparing the foundation and basement of the house. Once this foundation has been laid, the rest of the house goes up fairly quickly.

When Peter was preaching to the Jews, it was like building a house, knowing that the foundation was already there. Peter didn't have to spend time building the foundation. He could go straight to the structure to be built on the foundation. I believe that this was the situation generations ago in nations like America and England. Evangelists could assume a foundation upon which the gospel could stand. I also believe, however, there has been a major change — and the Church has sadly missed it.

Are our nations more like the model in Acts 2 — or are we in reality more like the very different situation in Acts 17?

A man who had attended the seminar in Caister a couple of years ago brought his wife to this year's meeting and she committed her life to the Lord. They purchased books, including *A Is for Adam* for their five-year-old boy, who committed his life to the Lord.

Also, a young married couple in Poole came up to me and told me they had both become Christians because of previous teaching they had heard at a seminar. They were so thankful as they stood there and told me how the Lord had used our ministry to convert both of them, that tears came to my eyes. The Lord is so good.

> (Ken Ham, sharing testimonies about people who attended AiG seminars in the United Kingdom.)

CHAPTER 5

THE CROSS — FOOLISHNESS!

> But we preach Christ crucified, unto the Jews
> a stumbling block, and unto the Greeks foolishness
> (1 Cor. 1:23).

In this section, we are going to look in detail at the meaning of the phrase, *"But we preach Christ crucified... unto the Greeks foolishness."*

At the beginning of Acts 17, we read a short account of Paul preaching to the Jews and Gentiles who were Jewish proselytes. Paul's approach is similar to that of Peter in Acts 2.

> Now when they had passed through Amphipolis
> and Apollonia, they came to Thessalonica, where was
> a synagogue of the Jews: And Paul, as his manner was,
> went in unto them, and three sabbath *days reasoned
> with them out of the scriptures,* Opening and alleging,
> that Christ must needs have suffered, and risen again
> from the dead; and that *this Jesus, whom I preach unto
> you, is Christ.* And some of them believed, and con-
> sorted with Paul and Silas; and of the devout Greeks
> a great multitude, and of the chief women not a few
> (Acts 17:1–4, emphasis added).

We note here that the focal point of his message was also that Jesus is Christ — in other words, the Messiah. Paul also *reasoned with them out of the Scriptures.* As in Acts 2, Paul, like Peter, could assume common ground in communicating the truth. The Jews and the Gentiles he was addressing had an understanding of the Old Testament Scriptures. To put it in more modern terms, it was enough for Paul to say "The Bible says. . . ."

In Acts 17:18–34, however, we are given an account of Paul preaching to a totally different culture, under completely different circumstances:

> Then certain *philosophers of the Epicureans, and of the Stoicks,* encountered him. And *some said, What will this babbler say? other some, He seemeth to be a setter forth of strange gods: because he preached unto them Jesus, and the resurrection.* And they took him, and brought him unto Areopagus, saying, May we know what this new doctrine, whereof thou speakest, is? For *thou bringest certain strange things to our ears*: we would know therefore what these things mean. (For all the Athenians and strangers which were there spent their time in nothing else, but either to tell, or to hear some new thing.)
>
> Then Paul stood in the midst of Mars' hill, and said, Ye men of Athens, I perceive that in all things ye are too superstitious. *For as I passed by, and beheld your devotions, I found an altar with this inscription, TO THE UNKNOWN GOD. Whom therefore ye ignorantly worship, him declare I unto you. God that made the world and all things therein, seeing that he is Lord of heaven and earth, dwelleth not in temples made with hands; Neither is worshipped with men's hands, as though he needed any thing, seeing he giveth to all life, and breath, and all things; And hath made of one blood all nations of men for to dwell on all the face of the earth, and hath determined the times before appointed, and the bounds of their habitation*; That they should seek the Lord, if haply they might feel after him, and find him, though he be not far from every one of us: For in him we live, and move, and have our being; as certain also of your own poets have said, For we are also his offspring.

Forasmuch then as we are the offspring of God, we ought not to think that the Godhead is like unto gold, or silver, or stone, graven by art and man's device. And the times of this ignorance God winked at; *but now commandeth all men every where to repent: Because he hath appointed a day, in the which he will judge the world in righteousness by that man whom he hath ordained; whereof he hath given assurance unto all men, in that he hath raised him from the dead. And when they heard of the resurrection of the dead, some mocked: and others said, We will hear thee again of this matter.*

So Paul departed from among them. *Howbeit certain men clave unto him, and believed*: among the which was Dionysius the Areopagite, and a woman named Damaris, and others with them (Acts 17:18–34, emphasis added).

This is a most fascinating passage of Scripture! There is much we can learn from Paul's approach here and apply it in our evangelistic efforts to reach the lost. Let's analyze this sermon carefully.

1. Who was Paul communicating with here? He was speaking to the Greek philosophers—the Epicureans and the Stoics. What did they believe about life? Did they have a different understanding of life compared to the Jews? It is well documented that these Greek philosophers were evolutionary-based in their thinking. Let me explain.

> **MANY PEOPLE TODAY HAVE THE WRONG IDEA ABOUT EVOLUTION. THEY THINK CHARLES DARWIN INVENTED THIS THEORY. BUT THIS IS SIMPLY NOT TRUE.**

Many people today have the wrong idea about evolution. They think Charles Darwin invented this theory. But this is simply not true. Darwin did popularize a particular view of evolution, but evolutionary ideas go way back in history.

The Epicureans taught that everything on the earth had evolved directly from the material of the earth itself. They didn't see any purpose in nature. For them, sensuous pleasure was the chief good of existence. The Stoics were pantheistic in their beliefs. Pantheism is just another form of evolutionism. Thus, the general thinking of the Greek culture was evolutionary. At the same time, however, they practiced idolatry. They believed in gods, but even the gods themselves evolved from some primordial substance.

The important thing to note here is that the Greek culture

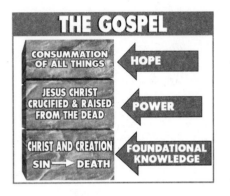

had no concept of the God the Jews believed in: a personal, infinite God who was responsible for, transcendent to, and an upholder of His creation. This thinking was totally missing from this culture.

One could say that when Paul was communicating to this culture, he was speaking to an evolution-based society. A knowledge of the real Creator was absent.

2. The Greeks did not have the Jewish Scriptures. Paul couldn't reason with them *out of the Scriptures*, as he (and Peter) did when speaking to those who were a part of the Jewish culture. The Greek culture was very complex with many different competing philosophies. While they saw "sin" and "evil" in their culture and recognized the importance of structure and laws, they had no concept of an absolute authority, absolute truth, or the inherent sin nature of man.

3. The Greeks had no understanding concerning their first ancestor, Adam, and the concept of original sin — nor had they received the law of Moses. Therefore, these people could not understand or accept the absolute authority of the Creator God, the lawgiver.

Consider again the three major elements of the gospel in this illustration. The Greeks listening to Paul on Mars Hill in Athens did not have the foundational knowledge to understand the gospel. To use our analogy from the last chapter, trying to get the Greeks to understand the gospel would be like attempting to build a skyscraper on the foundation of a small family home. The Greek culture had the wrong foundation. If a builder wanted to construct a skyscraper, he would have to first of all remove the wrong foundation. Then he would need to build the right foundation before the rest of the structure could be started.

This "wrong foundation" concept is clearly illustrated in the Greeks' response to the message of the Resurrection:

> And *some said, What will this babbler say? other some, He seemeth to be a setter forth of strange gods: because he preached unto them Jesus, and the resurrection.* And they took him, and brought him unto Areopagus, saying, *May we know what this new doctrine, whereof thou speakest, is? For thou bringest certain strange things to our ears* (Acts 17:18–20, emphasis added).

Their response went something like this: What foolishness is this? What strange tales are you telling us? What nonsense is this all about? Remember the statement in 1 Corinthians 1:23 that the preaching of the Cross was *foolishness* to the Greeks. It is very important to note at this stage that the reaction of the Greeks was very different to that of the Jews. Not all Jews accepted that Jesus

was the Messiah, of course, but large numbers did. And the rest understood what Paul and the others were telling them. The Greeks, however, had no concept of what this message of the Resurrection was all about. Paul couldn't appeal to the Scriptures to explain this message to them. So how was he going to get them to understand the message of the Cross — the power of the gospel?

In Romans Paul tells us the following:

> For the invisible things of him from the creation of the world are clearly seen, being understood by the things that are made, even his eternal power and God-head; so that they are without excuse (Rom. 1:20).

> Which shew the work of the law written in their hearts, their conscience also bearing witness (Rom. 2:15).

Even though pagan Greek philosophers had, by and large, obliterated the knowledge of the true God from their culture, Paul knew that he could appeal to nature and their consciences to begin to explain the concept of the true Creator God.

And so Paul began a great sermon as an apologetic (defense) to explain the Christian message from the foundation and upwards. Consider carefully the following four major elements in Paul's sermon.

1. Paul pointed to one (or more) of their own altars, reminding the Greeks that they had inscribed this (or these) to the *unknown god.* He began with some common ground from their own culture. He then set out to explain to them that this "unknown god" was in reality the true God. He carefully defined the nature of the true God. He emphasized that this was the Creator God — the One who made all things and upholds all things by His power.

This was in obvious contrast to their evolutionary and polytheistic views. Paul preached concerning the power of God in creation. (This passage reminds me of what my Japanese translator told me about how he had to define the word "God" when I used it in the Japanese culture that was devoid of a Christian basis.) Although this would have been a foreign concept to the Greeks,

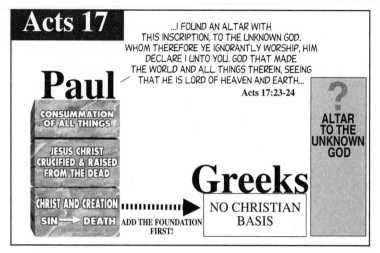

God's Word tells us that their own consciences and the creation itself are witnesses to this fact. And they were very interested in logic and logical arguments. God could use this powerful witness to open their hearts to the truth.

2. For people to understand that they are sinners, they also need to grasp the fact that we are all descendants of (and thus related to) the first man, Adam. Because he sinned, therefore we all sin: "Wherefore, as by one man sin entered into the world, and death by sin, and so death passed upon all men, for all have sinned" (Rom. 5:12). Thus Paul explained to the Greeks that we are all related (of one blood) and that we all are traced back to one man. Paul explained to them that God was in charge of the actions of the descendants of this one man — He was in charge of the nations. Nothing in any kingdom was beyond the control of God. The Greek culture was actually in the hand of God.

3. Paul also counteracted the Greeks' wrong religion. He spoke against their idols and explained to them that this Creator God was ruler and judge. And there was a Day of Judgment coming. He urged them to repent from their erroneous ways and believe in the true God.

4. Finally, Paul returned to the message of the Resurrection, the central part of the gospel. Paul didn't just stop with the message of creation, for this is not sufficient to bring salvation. However, he started with the preaching of God as the sovereign Creator,

> THE TRUTH OF THE MATTER IS THAT PAUL WAS *EXTREMELY* SUCCESSFUL, ESPECIALLY GIVEN THE CIRCUMSTANCES.

so that the Greeks would understand the message of salvation.

So after removing the wrong foundation from their thinking, and setting in the correct foundation, Paul then built the structure of the gospel, so that souls could be saved for eternity.

But was Paul really that successful using this approach? Acts 17:34 informs us that only a few believed. Surely one wouldn't describe this as a successful crusade! The truth of the matter is that Paul was *extremely* successful, especially given the circumstances. And this is the same sort of success that is needed today. The results of his preaching to the Greeks were actually astounding.

How could this be so?

My children and I attended your seminar in Seattle in October. After the grade school children's session, we introduced ourselves to you and you asked if our four year old, Timothy, had understood any of the lecture. I answered that I didn't know. I want you to know we later discovered how very much he did understand! My teenagers and I asked him every question we could think of and he knew it all!

Within two hours after the lecture, he showed his *D Is for Dinosaur* book to three people, two unsaved, and witnessed to an unsaved mom in a park, giving her the *Dinosaurs and the Bible* booklet you gave him. We followed up the seminar by reading to him various dinosaur books we purchased from your ministry. As a result of all this, Timothy accepted Jesus as his Lord and Savior! I really believe he understands and is truly saved!

B.K., Washington

CHAPTER 6

PIONEER EVANGELISM — OUTSTANDING SUCCESS!

Over the years, both in Australia and in America, I've had a number of Bible college and seminary students relate to me what some of their professors had declared concerning Paul's sermon in Acts 17. These professors said that Paul really failed in his approach at Athens because there were so few converts. He had tried to be too intellectual. What Paul should have done, they argued, was just boldly preach the message of sin and repentance as Peter did in Acts 2. The professors instructed the students not to adopt Paul's approach at Athens, but instead always pattern their evangelistic efforts after Peter's, outlined in Acts 2.

In actual fact, Paul was very successful in his Acts 17 sermon. Many people have missed the point that Paul was preaching to a culture that had the wrong foundation to understand the gospel. To communicate with such a culture, Paul had to change a whole way of thinking from the ground up. As we discussed in the previous chapter, it wasn't just a matter of presenting the message of the Cross and Resurrection; these people had to be given a whole new way to think before they could understand such a message.

What has helped me understand this point over the years is the fact that I have traveled widely and spoken in many different cultures. It has certainly been enlightening for me to realize how differently people from different cultures think. If a person has grown up in a country like Australia or the United States, but has not traveled outside those countries, they are more likely not to fully appreciate how different people's thought processes can be.

Can you imagine what it must be like when someone from India or Russia migrates to America? My own experience as an Australian living in America tells me that both Americans and the immigrants would have all sorts of miscommunications and misunderstandings because of the different ways of thinking each had.

I remember watching the movie comedy *The Gods Must Be Crazy,* which centered around an isolated tribe of bushmen in Africa. Someone in an airplane dropped a Coke bottle, which landed near this tribe. Because they hadn't seen such an object before, they didn't know what to do with it. Eventually, because of all the strife it caused, it was decided it was an evil thing that had to be disposed of. It was a humorous movie, yet it made the point that when something happens outside of our cultural experience, it can be very difficult to deal with.

A missionary I once spoke with told me that one day after reading Revelation 3:20 ("behold I stand at the door and knock"), the natives wanted to know why Jesus was a thief. He found out that in this culture, if someone stands at the door and knocks, they are a thief trying to come in and steal. However, if someone stands outside and calls out, then he is actually a friend coming to visit.

I can't emphasize enough the enormity of the task Paul had in communicating the truth of the gospel to the Greek culture. To understand more of what Paul had to do, we could liken Paul's work to that of a pioneer.

When the pioneers moved westward across America, they couldn't just set up camp, plant some seeds, and then reap a harvest. They first of all had to clear the land, then prepare the soil, plant the seed, and then they could obtain a harvest.

Consider the parable of the sower and the seed in Matthew 13:3–8:

> And he spake many things unto them in parables, saying, Behold, a sower went forth to sow; And when he sowed, some seeds fell by the way side, and the fowls came and devoured them up: Some fell upon stony places, where they had not much earth: and forthwith they sprung up, because they had no deepness of earth: And when the sun was up, they were scorched; and because they had no root, they withered away. And some fell among thorns; and the thorns sprung up, and choked them: But other fell into good ground, and brought forth fruit, some an hundredfold, some sixtyfold, some thirtyfold (Matt. 13:3–8).

There are, of course, many lessons that we can learn from this parable. However, notice that it was only when the seed fell in *good ground* that it could then bring *forth fruit*. When Paul went to the Greeks to sow the seed of the gospel, it was like sowing seeds *by the wayside* or on *stony ground*. Before the Greeks could understand the gospel, Paul had to prepare the ground — he had to construct the right foundation so the seed of the gospel could take root. Before he could successfully sow the seed, he first had to plow the ground!

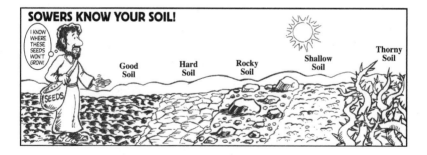

What Paul was involved in was *pre-evangelism* (or what I call "creation evangelism"). Mostly, we think of evangelism as sowing and reaping. Perhaps a pastor in a church sows the seed week after week, and then an evangelist is brought in and a harvest of souls is reaped. This, of course, works when the ground is already prepared to receive the seed as it was with the Jews. Christians, however, need to become familiar with the fact that it is becoming increasingly necessary to be involved in plowing first, then sowing, and finally reaping.

It should also be noted that this type of approach is slow and arduous. It takes much patience and hard work. But once the virgin soil is prepared, and the foundation is ready, then results will come much more quickly.

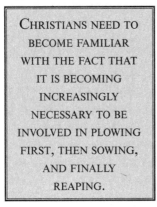

CHRISTIANS NEED TO BECOME FAMILIAR WITH THE FACT THAT IT IS BECOMING INCREASINGLY NECESSARY TO BE INVOLVED IN PLOWING FIRST, THEN SOWING, AND FINALLY REAPING.

Jeremiah 4:3 states, "For thus saith the Lord to the men of Judah and Jerusalem, Break up your fallow ground, and sow not among thorns."

One application we can make regarding this verse concerns the fact that the fallow ground cannot yield a crop until it is broken up (plowed) so that it can receive the seed. Even though it is a work of the Lord to "plow" people's hearts so they will be receptive to the gospel, nonetheless it is our responsibility to use our spiritual weapons in this spiritual battle:

> For the weapons of our warfare are not carnal, but mighty through God to the pulling down of strong holds; Casting down imaginations, and every high thing that exalteth itself against the knowledge of God, and bringing into captivity every thought to the obedience of Christ (2 Cor. 10:4–5).

Paul certainly excelled and thrived in pioneer evangelism. Although the results were rather small at first, churches were built and the Christian message reached the Gentiles. At the end of Paul's sermon on Mars Hill, we are told, "Howbeit certain men clave unto him, and believed: among the which was Dionysius the Areopagite, and a woman named Damaris, and others with them" (Acts 17:34).

There were some converts — people who changed their whole way of thinking. One cannot be critical of Paul because of the small number of converts. Instead, we should applaud this man who understood the need to work diligently at laying the foundation so the gospel could spread among the Gentiles, as it did so wonderfully. Churches were established, and God's Word began to spread throughout the world.

Many Christians have not thought about the concept of pioneer evangelism (or pre-evangelism). Or if they have, they usually think of this method as reserved for overseas missionaries ministering to some tribe of native people in a remote jungle.

As we shall see, however, pioneer evangelism must be adopted by the Church today, or there will be little plowed ground left for sowing the seed of the gospel. This is a necessary consequence of a foundational cultural change that has occurred in our Western nations. Did the Church miss this change? By and large, yes — because the Church, sadly, has actually helped bring this about! More about that in a moment. . . .

One of the ladies at church who ordered a set of seminar tapes told me a great success story this morning! After listening to the tapes, she sent them, along with an AiG catalog, to her daughter, who shared them with neighbors. As a result, two families, who previously belonged to a group who believed that Jesus was just a good man (a cult), now have changed their thinking because of AiG tapes and materials.

A.C., Colorado

CHAPTER 7

FROM "JEWS" — TO "GREEKS"

I t is my contention that countries like America, England, Australia, and other Western nations were in generations past, in a sense, like the "Jews." Thus, evangelists could approach them in the same way that Peter did in Acts 2. They had a Bible foundation. However, I believe that a foundational cultural change has occurred so that these nations are now like the "Greeks." Because the Church, by and large, has not recognized this change, effective evangelism is becoming increasingly rare.

A fascinating quotation appeared in the March 2002 issue of *Charisma* magazine. Publisher Stephen Strang, who probably personally knows more missionaries and evangelists than anyone else, was writing about efforts to reach the world with the gospel of Jesus Christ: "And calls for world evangelism seem to have little long-term effect."

This amazing frankness, coming from the Pentecostal world (who are among the most passionate people about soul winning that the world has ever seen) illustrates the difficulty faced today by Christians who spend enormous amounts of energy, time, and money to fulfill the Great Commission.

Over the years I have visited many countries. I have lived in Australia and America, and have spent considerable time in

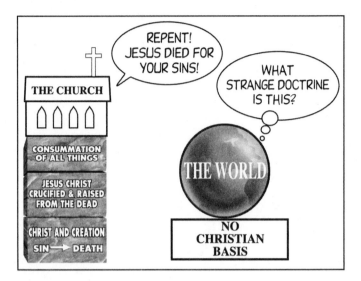

England. I therefore want to relate to you just some of the many observations I have made concerning these three countries. I then want to apply these observations to evangelism.

AUSTRALIA

In 1959, when I was just a small boy, I vividly remember a major event in Australia's history. A famous evangelist, known then as "The Bible Says Man," came to Australia for a series of crusades. Now, Australia is not — and never has been — a Christian country to any great extent. Americans often tell me that their country began with founding fathers who had great convictions. I tell them that Australia's founding fathers also had great "convictions," but of a different sort! Of course, Australia began as a penal settlement for convicts sent from England over 200 years ago.

At the same time, the Christian philosophy that pervaded the English culture also was incorporated to some degree in Australian culture. When this evangelist visited Australia, the whole of Australia seemed to be buzzing. Most people were aware of what was happening. Communication lines were set up across the country to transmit his voice on loudspeakers. I recall going to a church hall and sitting in front of a big speaker as this evangelist preached.

His main message could be likened to that of Peter in Acts 2. He called people to repentance. And it is true that thousands were convicted of their sin and repented. Some historians have claimed that this is the closest Australia ever came to revival. I know of people in Christian leadership in Australia today who were converted during that particular crusade.

But here is a very important comparison: When that same evangelist came back in 1969, 1979, and by satellite linkup in the 1990s, with the same message (of sin and repentance), he didn't get anywhere *near* the same response. Australia did not "buzz" as it did in the 1950s. Certainly, some people went forward. However, like many crusades today, if we are really honest, there are few real first-time commitments compared to what happened generations ago. Something was different. (Incidentally, when this same evangelist went to Singapore in 1971, the response was similar to that in Australia in 1959. What is of interest is that Singapore had not yet introduced evolution into any of its curricula.)

My father was a public school principal in the state of Queensland. In accord with Education Department regulations, my father would have prayer each day with all the public school students before they went to their classes. Also, each teacher at the beginning of class was required to read a Bible story for that day.

I would say that most students were very aware of the Bible, and familiar with many of its passages, such as Adam and Eve, Noah, Jesus' birth and death and resurrection, and so on. They were certainly familiar with the Ten Commandments and understood Christian morality. They had a sense of what was right and wrong.

However, here is an important observation: Public schools in Australia today do not have prayer or Bible readings as part of their daily schedule. Although ministers of religion are allowed to conduct religious education classes, the system as a whole has actually now become very anti-Christian.

As a teacher in the public school system in the 1970s, I was always thrilled when the Gideons came to hand out free Bibles

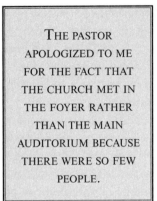

THE PASTOR APOLOGIZED TO ME FOR THE FACT THAT THE CHURCH MET IN THE FOYER RATHER THAN THE MAIN AUDITORIUM BECAUSE THERE WERE SO FEW PEOPLE.

(New Testaments with Psalms and Proverbs) to all the students. I noticed, however, that as time went on, an increasing number of students refused to take one of these free Bibles. Something was definitely causing a change in attitude to the Bible.

In countries like Canada, the Gideons are no longer allowed to give out free Bibles in public schools. In Australia, although Gideons are still permitted to hand out Bibles in public schools, there are some individual school councils who no longer allow this. Things are changing.

ENGLAND

As an Australian, I had always thought of England as being rather Christian. After all, this is the home of Bunyan, Spurgeon, Whitefield, Wesley, and others. Yet, I was shocked the first time I traveled to England. There was hardly any vestige of Christianity left in public life. Conservative Bible-believing churches were mostly small and struggling. As I traveled across the country I noticed old churches that were converted into antique stores or even mosques.

On more than one occasion, I found myself preaching in a church that once held thousands of people, but now only a few dozen members attended. At one place, the pastor apologized to me for the fact that the church met in the foyer rather than the main auditorium because there were so few people.

And yet, before the last world war, church attendance in England made up a considerable percentage of the population (perhaps as much as 40–50 percent). Now, church attendance is more like 5 percent! Something has happened to the Church in England.

UNITED STATES OF AMERICA

The first time I came to America, in the early 1980s, I was astonished at how "Christian" this country seemed to be. By comparison, until recent times, there were no Christian radio stations in Australia — I couldn't believe the fact I could listen to Christian stations all across the nation. To me it was almost as unbelievable to see the number of churches in cities and towns all across the United States. In Australia, church attendance is quite low (probably around 5 percent for regular attendees). To me, America was very Christian.

I was startled to see nativity scenes in public places, but have noticed over the years how these are being gradually removed as court cases — often instigated by humanist organizations — challenge such displays. A change was occurring.

Considering how Christian America appeared to be, I was also shocked to find out that prayer was no longer allowed to be supported by officials in public schools. In fact, prayer, Bible readings, and the Ten Commandments (God's law) seem to be all but outlawed now in schools across the country. I understand a lot of this change started in the 1960s. (Now it is true that the First Amendment of the U.S. Constitution does guarantee students free expression regarding their Christian beliefs, but because of intimidation by humanist groups, most school officials are reluctant to even consider this.) The U.S. Supreme Court has now interpreted the First Amendment — as far as teachers are concerned — to mean that they are not allowed to be seen to impose the Christian view above any other.

In recent times in America, public schools have been suffering from violence, drugs, and sexual perversion. It's sad to note that at school conferences there are now booths selling the latest in metal detectors, X-ray machines, and the like, to help curb problems on the school grounds. There is no doubt — great changes have occurred all around in America.

GENERAL OBSERVATIONS

I would also like make a few other general observations concerning all three countries.

It is becoming increasingly difficult to get people to attend church. Many churches have now resorted to expensive programs to attract people. It seems to be getting harder to bridge the gap between the Church and the world.

Most of those who attend crusades or revival meetings today already have a church background. There certainly are conversions, but compared to generations ago, the number of really sincere first-time commitments (in most instances) is really quite small. By and large, the unchurched are becoming more difficult to reach.

Generations ago, in all three countries, many parents automatically sent their children to Sunday school or church programs, even if they themselves did not attend church. Increasingly, though, more and more families do not send their children to such events.

In all these countries, we observe increasing lawlessness, suicide, abortion, homosexual behavior, pornography, euthanasia, and many other social ills. The Christian framework once prevalent in these nations is collapsing. Christian morality is waning. Increasingly, people don't have a sense of right and wrong on many issues that were once clear-cut in generations past (e.g., sex, adultery, pornography). For instance, in the United States, morality and character were once vital criteria in presidential elections. In 1998, however, it was evident from how the public viewed the moral crisis in the White House that this was no longer so. So what has happened to these nations? What has caused these changes?

Generations ago, I believe these (and other Western nations) were like the "Jews." Prayer, Bible readings, and God's law were even a part of the public education system. Most people understood (and basically accepted) Christian morality. People understood the concept of the Creator God of the Bible. They knew what was meant by sin, and accepted absolutes. When an evangelist preached a message of sin and repentance, people could be pricked in their hearts (as the hearers were in Acts 2). They knew that sin was adultery, sexual perversion, lying, stealing, and not loving God with all their heart.

The founding fathers of America understood what would happen if Christianity (including prayer and the Bible) were ever taken out of the education system. For instance, one of the signers of the Declaration of Independence stated:

The only foundation for a useful education in a republic is to be laid in religion. Without this there can be no virtue, and without virtue there can be no liberty, and liberty is the object and life of all republican governments. Without religion, I believe that learning does real mischief to the morals and principles of mankind.[1]

The present fashionable practice of rejecting the Bible from our schools, I suspect, has originated with the Deists. They discover great ingenuity in this new mode of attacking Christianity. If they proceed in it, they will do more in half a century in extirpating our religion than [anti-religious philosophers] Bollingbroke or Voltaire could have effected in a thousand years.[2]

The Bible, when not read in schools, is seldom read in any subsequent period of life.[3]

At the time of the Reformation in the 16th century, the world was a "dark" place. People lived in fear, and superstition abounded. The Word of God was suppressed and not generally available. Church leaders insisted they were the only ones to determine what God's Word meant. Luther led the Reformation to get people back to the sure Word of God and to get the Scriptures into the hands of the average person. What a change this wrought. We are still reaping the effects of this Reformation today. But sadly, as the Church compromises the Word of God with the teachings of fallible men — and as more and more highly educated Christian leaders insist that only they can really interpret and give meaning to the Scriptures for the average person —we are seeing a reversal today of the Reformation that brought such light to a dark world.

Luther's warning concerning education in the 16th century is more pertinent than ever today:

The universities only ought to turn out men who are experts in the Holy Scriptures, men who can become bishops and priests, and stand in the front and all the world. But where do you find that? I greatly fear that the universities, unless they teach the Holy Scriptures diligently and impress them on the young students, are wide gates to hell.[4]

Luther added:

I would advise no one to send his child where the Holy Scriptures are not supreme. Every institution that does not unceasingly pursue the study of God's Word becomes corrupt. Because of this we can see what kind of people they become in the universities and what they are like now.[5]

When the Bible (and thus Christianity) was the foundational basis of a nation, there was much plowed ground, prepared for the seed to be planted. I suggest that this is why evangelists in generations past could reap such wonderful harvests. The Christian gospel could be communicated, for most people had the same way of thinking. They all started from the same basic presuppositions.

What has happened is that increasingly these cultures have now become like the "Greeks." They have, by and large, lost the Christian foundation that once existed. We have generations of people who have been trained in an education system basically devoid of the knowledge of God.

Most of the Church is still approaching these cultures as if they are "Jews" — but they are not. They are becoming more like the "Greeks" each day. And if the Church doesn't wake up to this change, increasingly they will not make a major impact on the culture, and any vestige of a Christian fabric that still exists will be all but lost.

What happened to bring about this change? What is the root cause? And why hasn't the Church understood this change if it has occurred?

The Church, to a large degree, has helped the change, because the Church itself has changed to being more like the "Greeks." This is the fundamental problem with our Western cultures today.

The Church Today

THIS IS THE WAY WE'VE ALWAYS SPREAD
THE GOSPEL IN THE PAST. WOW! THESE WEEDS
ARE GETTING WORSE EVERY DAY! OH WELL!

And this is where the real cause lies in regard to the collapse of
Christianity in the West.

Even as an unbeliever, I had at least been exposed
to what God's Word said about His creation during

Sunday school. I remember sitting in public school listening to evolutionary theory being taught as fact and thinking, *That can't be! How could these living things just change?* I was an unbeliever at the time, but nonetheless, I was really skeptical about evolution.

As I continued on in public school, I was, of course, systematically and continually exposed to evolutionary concepts. I finally "gave in" and instead of trying to argue against evolution, I began trying to reconcile evolution with the Bible. The saddest part is that my pastor did not have an answer for my questions based on the Scriptures. This was 20 years ago, and I fear the situation is much worse today.

I am very encouraged by and grateful for the work your organization is doing to stand up for the truth and reliability of God's Word. I now homeschool my two daughters and rely a great deal on your magazine and other books you publish to teach them about God's Word and His world. I also give your books away as Christmas presents to my husband's brothers and their families. They are all "heaped and steeped" in evolutionary thought, and we pray that God would bring these families to the whole truth of His Word.

M.G., Colorado

CHAPTER **8**

THE EVOLUTION CONNECTION

W hen I was teaching in the public schools in Australia, I certainly made no secret about the fact that I was a born-again Christian. What I noticed, though, was that some students would scoff at me for believing in the Bible, because the teaching of evolution had convinced them the Bible wasn't true.

During my years as a teacher, and many times since then as I have spoken around the world, I've had people use evolution as their excuse as to why the Bible couldn't be trusted. In fact, I've found that evolution is one of the biggest, if not *the* biggest, stumbling block to people being receptive to the gospel of Jesus Christ.

I have many letters of testimony on file from people who admit that it was after they were shown that evolution was not scientific fact that the Lord opened their heart to the truth of His Word (see chapter 14 for examples of such testimonies).

The situation I detailed in chapter 1 concerning the Australian pastors and their problem of communicating with students back in

> SOME STUDENTS WOULD SCOFF AT ME FOR BELIEVING IN THE BIBLE, BECAUSE FOR THEM THE TEACHING OF EVOLUTION CONVINCED THEM THE BIBLE WASN'T TRUE.

1975 really sums up a major problem with which the Church needs to grapple today.

Many Christians, including most Christian leaders, don't understand the connection of evolution to the social ills of our culture and the difficulties in getting people interested in Christianity. They see evolution as something totally separate from such issues. I think the main reason for this misunderstanding is because many Christians have been indoctrinated to believe that evolution is factual science.

Now, I taught real science as a teacher. I taught students about computers, chemical reactions, the technology that put man on the moon, and so on. But I also taught them that when a person talks about origins — about the past — they have just stepped outside of the science they use in everyday life. Evolution is a belief about the past. (There are a number of books I highly recommend to study this issue.[1])

It is true that most evolutionary scientists, the media, and the average public school textbook today present atheistic (perhaps subtly rather than overtly) evolution as fact. Students are taught that the universe and all life arose by strictly material causes. God is not given any place in the "origin of anything." Over the years, the teaching of evolution has intensified in our school systems and through the media. So much so that the average person believes that scientists have proved the earth is billions of years old and that the different forms of life arose through an evolutionary process of death and struggle.

For instance, consider this 1993 quote from the widely read *Natural History* magazine:

> As for the claim that evolution is an unproved theory, that's nonsense. Evolution is a fact, established with the same degree of confidence as our "theory" of disease, and the atomic "theory" of matter. Yes, there is lively debate about the particular evolutionary mechanisms that caused particular changes, but the existence of evolutionary change is not in doubt. Our own bodies provide walking evidence.[2]

What most evolutionists really think is summed up by Harvard geneticist Richard Lewontin in his review of Sagan's *Billions and Billions of Demons:*

> We take the side of science in spite of the absurdity of some of its constructs, in spite of its failure to fulfill many of its extravagant promises of health and life, in spite of the tolerance of the scientific community for unsubstantiated just-so stories, because we have a prior commitment, a commitment to materialism. It is not that the methods and institutions of science somehow compel us to accept a material explanation of the phenomenal world, but, on the contrary, that we are forced by our *a priori* adherence to material causes to create an apparatus of investigation and a set of concepts that produce material explanations, no matter how mystifying to the uninitiated. Moreover, that *materialism is absolute, for we cannot allow a Divine Foot in the door*[3] [emphasis ours].

And in 1998, the prestigious National Academy of Sciences made a book available to public schools and colleges to help teachers further indoctrinate students in evolution. In this book, which was to be used by many in the public education system, we read how the academy wants public school students to be taught:

> The theory of evolution explains how life on earth has changed. In scientific terms, "theory" does

not mean "guess" or "hunch" as it does in everyday usage. Scientific theories are explanations of natural phenomena built up logically from testable observations and hypotheses. Biological evolution is the best scientific explanation we have for the enormous range of observations about the living world. Scientists most often use the word "fact" to describe an observation. But scientists can also use fact to mean something that has been tested or observed so many times that there is no longer a compelling reason to keep testing or looking for examples. *The occurrence of evolution in this sense is a fact*[4] [emphasis ours].

Now think about this connection: The more that generations of students are indoctrinated to believe in solely material causes for the origin of life — and the more their thinking processes are devoid of any understanding of a Creator God — the more they are led to believe that there are no absolutes and truth is relative, what will ultimately happen?

Well, consider what the humanists say will happen:

The day will come when the evidence constantly accumulating around the evolutionary theory becomes so massively persuasive that even the last and most fundamental Christian warriors will have to lay down their arms and surrender unconditionally. I believe that day will be the end of Christianity.[5]

The more evolutionary ideas pervade the culture, the more a person's whole way of thinking will change. For them, right and wrong will be whatever they determine for themselves, if they can get away with it. If they are just an animal, then no one owns them, so their body is their own. Thus, why can't they do what they want with sex? Also, if this life is all there is, and death ends it all, then if things get tough, why

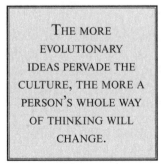

THE MORE EVOLUTIONARY IDEAS PERVADE THE CULTURE, THE MORE A PERSON'S WHOLE WAY OF THINKING WILL CHANGE.

not commit suicide now and get out of it — after all, a person won't remember they ever had life, so what's the point anyway? And, if we get rid of spare animals by killing them, then what's wrong with getting rid of spare babies by abortion?

Now, don't get me wrong here. People are not stupid. They are just being consistent with their presuppositions. Hitler was not silly. Some even say in some ways he was a genius, albeit he was warped in his thinking. But he consistently applied what he believed about origins. This led to the deaths of millions of people. Abortionists today are not intellectually inferior. They are just being consistent with their presuppositions, the foundation they ultimately have for their thinking.

I read an article recently about a famous Christian leader discussing the school violence problem in America. A number of recent situations have occurred where students have killed teachers, fellow students, and even their parents. This man of God concentrated on abuse in childhood as a major contributing factor to these killings. Now while I agree that this is a complicated issue, and certainly child abuse leads to all sorts of problems, the overall problem I believe is *much* deeper than this.

Some people misunderstand me when I say there's a connection between evolution and these social ills mentioned above. I'm *not* saying that evolution is the cause of abortion or school violence. What I am saying is that the more a culture abandons God's Word as the absolute authority, and the more a culture accepts an evolutionary philosophy, then the way people think, and their attitudes, will also change. I'm not saying that a student says to himself, "Now, I'm just an animal — I know evolution is true — therefore there's no basis for right or wrong — so there's nothing to stop me from shooting my teacher."

But what has happened is that the thinking of generations of people has gradually changed so that they don't think in a Christian framework anymore. Their presuppositions are different. They approach life with a different philosophy, and thus their actions result in abortion, school violence, child abuse, sexual perversion, and so on. Now take abuse: this fuels the fire and accelerates these existing presuppositions to their natural conclusions, and young people become angry inside. Because of this "mental pain," they can justify all sorts of wrongful actions.

Now it is true that people who don't believe in evolution can do these same sinful things. But, the more people abandon a Christian basis, the more these ills will become prevalent throughout the whole of society. The restraining influence of absolute authority starts to dissipate.

The following diagram best sums up what I see as the major problem in our Western nations today:

Let's consider this diagram in some detail.

On the right we see the castle of Christianity (representing doctrines such as sin, marriage, salvation, etc.), which is founded on the proposition: "God's Word is Truth." Under this is the word "creation." It's important to note that ultimately, all biblical doctrines of theology are founded in the creation account of Genesis 1–11.[6] In Matthew 19:4–6, when Jesus Christ was asked about marriage, he immediately quoted from Genesis 1:27 and

2:24 to explain the doctrine of marriage as one man for one woman for life.

> And he answered and said unto them, Have ye not read, that he which made them at the beginning made them male and female, And said, For this cause shall a man leave father and mother, and shall cleave to his wife: and they twain shall be one flesh? Wherefore they are no more twain, but one flesh. What therefore God hath joined together, let not man put asunder (Matt. 19:4–6).

Thus, Jesus believed Genesis as real history. If you think about it, if Genesis is just an allegory, or mythological, then marriage can be defined any way you want. The historical fact that God made man from dust and then a woman from man's side is the only reason marriage (being that of a male and female) can be defended. Jesus and Paul (Eph. 5) taught that a couple become one in marriage.

This oneness is based on the historical fact that Eve was created out of Adam's side. Sadly, there are many Christians who believe that God used the evolutionary process to form life and finally man. However, the evolutionary story has the man descended from an "ape-man" and the woman descending from an "ape-woman." If, as some Christians insist, God then created souls for this evolved man and woman, then the doctrine of marriage has been destroyed. Only a literal Genesis has the woman being made *from* the man, and this is the only basis of oneness in marriage.

As we mentioned in chapter 2, if the fall of man was not a literal event involving a literal man, serpent, garden, tree, and fruit, then sin can be defined any way you want. My book *The Lie: Evolution*[7] deals with this issue (and with all major Christian doctrines) in much more detail. Suffice it to say that if Genesis is not accepted as literal history, then there is no foundation for any Christian doctrine to stand upon.

On the left of the castle diagram, the castle of humanism, and the social issues of abortion, homosexual behavior, etc., are built on the foundation of "man's opinions determine truth." Under this is the word "evolution." I need to define here what I mean by evolution. Most people think of the molecules-to-man belief that Darwin popularized. Although this is certainly a part of evolution, I believe we need to realize that evolution per se is much more than this. In essence, *it is a philosophy of life which teaches that man, independent of God and independent of revelation, determines truth.* Thus, man's opinions determine truth.

Humanism, of course, is a religion that teaches that man is the measure of all things. There is no supernatural being to whom we are accountable. Man can then decide truth for himself. The evolutionary teaching that man has evolved as a higher animal is a part of the *Humanist Manifesto,* for this is foundational to the religion of humanism.

> Religious humanists regard the universe as self-existing and not created. . . . Humanism believes that man is a part of nature and that he has emerged as the result of a continuous process. . . . Humanism recognizes that man's religious culture and civilization, as clearly depicted by anthropology and history, are the product of a gradual development due to his interaction with his natural environment and with his social heritage.[8]

> As non-theists, we begin with humans not God, nature not deity. Nature may indeed be broader and deeper than we know; any new discoveries, however, will but enlarge our knowledge of the natural.[9]

Logically, then, the more a person believes he is not special, but just an animal (and therefore driven by instinct and impulse), the more he will believe that he can decide truth for himself. The more he believes there is no God (absolute authority) to whom he is accountable, the more he can consistently decide right and wrong for himself. He will thus yield to the desires of the flesh. So, why shouldn't he conclude that marriage be two men — or why bother with marriage at all?

These two castles, then, represent a battle: The battle between the humanist world view and the Christian world view.

At a foundational level, this battle is between man determining truth for himself and God's Word being the ultimate truth. Or, it can be summarized as creation (God's Word is truth) versus evolution (man's opinions determine truth).

Look closely at how this battle is portrayed. The humanists are seen as very clever. They have aimed their guns at the foundations of Christianity. They have attacked the authority of the Word of God. There is no doubt that they've been successful in undermining the Word of God in our Western culture. But how have they done this? They have directly attacked the foundational book of the Bible — Genesis.

Through the education system, the media, the movies — through all the culture — evolutionary thinking is all pervasive. Creation versus evolution is NOT a side issue. They are really the front lines of the battle.

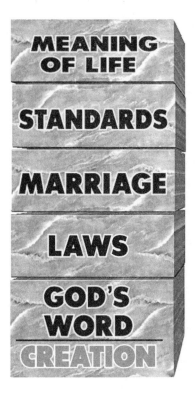
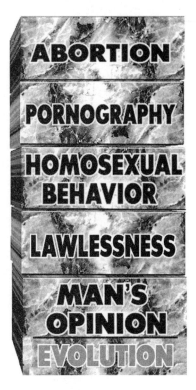

Now, read the description of this battle as seen through the eyes of a humanist:

> I am convinced that the battle for humankind's future must be waged and won in the public school classroom by teachers who correctly perceive their role as the proselytizers of a new faith: a religion of humanity that recognizes and respects the spark of what theologians call divinity in every human being. These teachers must embody the same selfless dedication as the most rabid fundamentalist preachers, for they will be ministers of another sort, utilizing a classroom instead of a pulpit to convey humanist values in whatever subject they teach, regardless of the educational level—preschool day care or large state university. The classroom must and will become an arena of conflict between the old and the new — the rotting corpse of Christianity, together with all its adjacent evils and misery, and the new faith of humanism.[10]

Most of Christendom has succumbed to the attacks at this foundational level. Most Christian leaders have allowed the teachings of evolution to one degree or another to be added to the Bible. They haven't understood that this has undermined the authority of the Bible.

For instance, most Christian leaders have accepted that the earth is billions of years old.[11] Yet, clearly from the words of Scripture alone, God created the universe in six literal days.[12] Christian leaders admit this, but they believe that scientists have proved the age of the earth to be billions of years. Therefore, they believe the days should be reinterpreted. In doing so, they have just allowed the authority of the Bible to be undermined. If the words of the Bible mean six days, but can't because of so-called science, then it means that the Bible is fallible! If we can't trust the words in Genesis, where do we start trusting the words and why?

I believe that humanists relish this compromise by Christian leaders. For instance, a Christian teacher friend attended a

"Teaching Evolution" seminar for public school teachers. This seminar was designed to help teachers in public schools teach evolution more effectively. At one stage of the discussion, the question came up regarding what they should do with students who are Christians. One of the leading spokespersons for humanism in America gave the following reply (as summed up in my friend's letter to me):

> The teachers were advised to suggest to the Bible-believers to consult their clergy, who would usually assure them that belief in evolution is OK!!![13]

What a sad indictment on the Church! The humanists use the compromising Christian leaders to further their cause to undermine the foundations of Christianity.

I believe this is what happened: The older generations in the Church allowed the teaching of evolution and/or millions of years to be added to the Bible. They didn't realize the true nature of what was happening. Most of these people believed the Bible to be the infallible, inerrant Word of God. They just added evolutionary teaching (e.g., millions of years of history) to this. But the next generation then grew up already disbelieving Genesis. This, I'm convinced, has led to generations in the Church being skeptical about the Bible's teaching in many other areas. They lost a sense of absolutes.

As just one example of what has happened to the younger generation, the following quote from a student at a well-known Christian college says it all:

> We cannot read the Bible by itself and expect to understand its messages. Instead, we need to apply rational thought and research to our biblical studies. . . . One way of seeking truth is by questioning the Bible. . . . Perhaps it would be better to read it as it was intended to be read, as a variety of texts intended to reveal God's unchanging truth to ancient cultures. Because the Bible was not directly addressed to our culture, it is important that we read it in its proper context instead of deifying it by reading it literally.[14]

Let me add something very important here. There are many Christian leaders who do not believe in evolution as such, but they do accept billions of years for the age of the earth — and millions of years for the formation of fossil layers. These people will call themselves creationists — and they are, in the sense that they don't believe in chance, random processes to produce life. Many of them don't even believe that God used an evolutionary process. But they have accepted that there were millions of years of death, disease, and suffering before Adam.

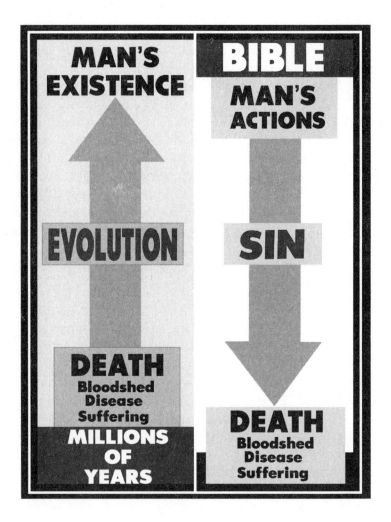

Now, when a Christian believes that the death, bloodshed, disease, suffering, and violence in the fossil record represents millions of years of history as God "created," then what did sin do to the world? What did the Curse do? Why does death have anything to do with sin? Why does God describe this as *very good*? Does that mean violence and disease are "good" in God's eyes? Is it any wonder young people today have no sense of sin and the holiness of God? I have written a number of articles explaining this important matter in detail.[15]

> WITH SO MUCH ENERGY AND MONEY EXPENDED IN THE FIGHT FOR CHRISTIAN MORALITY, WHY ARE CHRISTIANS LOSING THE BATTLE?

Look at the castle diagram again and notice how the Christians usually fight the battle. They don't really understand that their foundation is being shot out from under them. They know there's a problem. Yes, they see the social ills and they're concerned about the increasing problems of abortion, pornography, homosexual behavior, and all the other evils. But they don't realize that the change has occurred *foundationally*. Thus, they aim their guns at each other – or fire into nowhere – or shoot at their own foundation (when they believe in evolution and/or millions of years), or merely shoot at the issues.

This is a major problem in Christendom. Too many people concentrate solely on fighting the issues, when the issues are not the problem. They are simply the *symptoms* of the real problem.

I believe this was born out in America in the 1998 election results. Many Christians expected a real backlash against the president because of his admission of a moral failure. Christians were perplexed and despondent, however, when the election results indicated that the population as a whole was not concerned about morality as an issue.

In fact, if we are really honest, the Church is losing America. The once-Christian moral fabric is in tatters, and is getting worse every day. And yet, billions of dollars have been donated to major Christian organizations that have been fighting issues like abortion, homosexual behavior, pornography, and the destruction of the family. With so much energy and money expended in the fight for Christian morality, why are Christians losing the battle?

I believe it's because these organizations have not understood the real nature of what has happened. The main reason is because they themselves (regardless of the other good things they are doing) are not ultimately involved in proclaiming the Word of God as truth, beginning with Genesis. They are not fighting the humanists at the very place where humanists have attacked the Bible.

Personally, I believe that Christian leaders and Christians in general come across to the culture as being judgmental. This is because the Christians are insisting that these social ills (abortion, etc.) are wrong — and that is true. But they are only wrong if the Bible is true! And this is the problem: the culture as a whole doesn't view the Bible as the absolute authority any more. And sadly, most of the Church doesn't either, because they have allowed man's beliefs (e.g., millions of years, etc.) to be a judge on Scripture. Until the Church and these Christian organizations recognize this, my prediction is that increasingly, despite all the billions of dollars spent by Christians in fighting social ills, the nation will actually become more anti-Christian every day.

Many Christians (and non-Christians who hold a Christian morality) are becoming frustrated. Some people are resorting to violence because they don't see any real change occurring. But it's not the fighting of the issues or resorting to violence that will stem the tide of the secularization of society. The answer is so basic — and it's the same answer Martin Luther gave back in the 16th century. When Luther opposed the Roman Catholic Church over the issue of justification by faith, some followers wanted to resort to violence to settle the issue. How did Luther respond? Read this excerpt from a book on the history of Protestantism:

> Ulrich of Hutten . . . also offered himself as a champion of the Reformer. His mode of warfare, however, differed from Luther's. Ulrich was for falling

on Rome with the sword; Luther sought to subdue her by the weapon of Truth.

"It is with sword and with bows," wrote Ulrich, "with javelins and bombs that we must crush the fury of the devil." "I will not have recourse to arms and bloodshed in defense of the gospel," said Luther, shrinking back from the proposal. *"It was by the Word that the Church was founded and by the Word also it shall be re-established."*[16]

Yet, in our time, the Word has been compromised, and thus the Church has lost her weapon that can bring victory.

What has happened is that there's been a foundational change in our culture. This is what most of the Church has missed, mainly because most of the Church has compromised in some way with some or all of evolutionary teaching anyway. Even those Christians who have rejected evolutionary teaching and millions of years often don't understand the foundational connection of Genesis to Christian doctrine or the foundational connection of evolution to humanism and our social ills as pictured in the illustration:

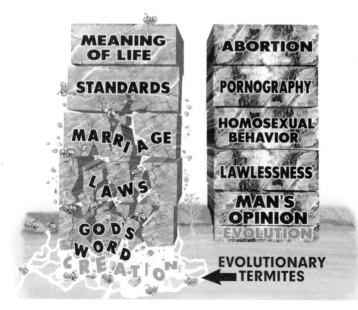

87

This foundational change from God's Word (creation) to man's opinions (evolution) is the change I referred to as from being like the "Jews" to being like the "Greeks."

Let me illustrate this practically for you. Look again at the right side of the castle diagram. Generations ago, when the Bible was really the foundation of the American culture, and someone preached about sin, people understood what was meant. They had the right foundation. However, because America has changed its foundation (now look to the foundation on the left — man's opinions/evolution), when a person preaches about sin and because the culture has a different foundation, then he doesn't understand what this is all about. People today don't think the same way as previous generations did with the other foundation. It's a *different* culture.

Let me give you another example. When America had the foundation on the right of the illustration (God's Word is truth — creation), then when someone said "abortion is wrong," on this former foundation a person would say, "Yes, you are right. Abortion is sin."

Because the culture has changed its foundation to "man's opinions determine truth" (evolution), then when the same message is preached, "abortion is wrong," the answer is more like this: "What are you talking about? I have a right to do what I want with my body. We're just animals anyway. No one has a right to tell me what to do."

I want to also illustrate for you how this battle applies in the average church situation. Most Sunday school and Christian school (or equivalent) literature concentrates on teaching Bible stories. Now, these stories are important. My parents taught them to me. But this is what is happening today: in our churches we teach Bible *stories* — Jonah and the whale — Jesus' death and resurrection — the feeding of the five thousand — Noah's ark — and so on. But the children then go out into the world. Most go to public schools, watch secular television, and read newspapers and magazines.

And what is the world saying to them? That you can't trust the Bible. Science has proved the Bible wrong, they say. Anyway,

Noah couldn't get all the animals on the ark — it's just a fairy tale. Dinosaurs prove evolution is true. Humans evolved from "ape-men" — the story of Adam and Eve is a fairy tale. There's no evidence of God's existence. And you can't answer questions like, "Where did Cain get his wife?"

And how do churches respond? They just keep teaching Bible stories.

Lest we think that it's only been liberal churches who have accepted evolutionary presuppositions about Genesis, note *The Message of Genesis,* a 1961 book by Ralph H. Elliot (published by the Southern Baptists' Sunday School Board):

> One can say with [Alan] Richardson: "We must learn to think of the stories of Genesis — the creation, the Fall, Noah's ark, the Tower of Babel . . . in the same way as we think of the parables of Jesus; they are profoundly symbolical (although not allegorical) stories, which aren't to be taken as literally true. . . ."

Since the 19th century, church leaders have embraced the proponents of atheistic naturalism, and today many of them walk hand in hand.

For years and years, humanists have slowly but surely taken over the thinking of the culture. While they were eroding the foundations of Christianity, the Church kept on just teaching Bible stories, without answering the attacks of the critics of the Bible.

The Church has expected each generation to continue believing these Bible stories, when each successive generation has been given increasing doses of evolutionary teaching attacking the Bible's historicity, particularly in the Book of Genesis, the foundational book of the entire Bible.

So now, not only is the culture as a whole more like the "Greeks" than the "Jews," but we also have generations of people in our churches who have been trained to think like "Greeks." They may believe the Bible stories, but they don't understand why they believe what they do. They don't know what to do about the collapsing Christian culture — they see the issues, but not the foundational problem, because they've had the foundation removed from their own thinking.

To most Christians today, the Bible is separate from the real world — it doesn't really connect. They don't understand that the Bible must be foundational to *all* of our thinking. They don't think with a Christian world view — they really have a secular philosophy. That's why when confronted with topics like dinosaurs, most shrug their shoulders. They don't know what to say. They haven't been trained to think in terms of the Bible being a history book that outlines when animals were made — what they ate before sin — how death entered the world — that animals, like dinosaurs, got on a boat, and so on. My book, *The Great Dinosaur Mystery Solved,* offers details on how to develop this Christian world view and apply it in the real world.[17]

The world has attacked Christianity at a foundational level, and the Church has for the most part just continued teaching Bible stories. Christians need to be trained to believe God's Word from Genesis to Revelation, and know how to defend it. But we are commanded to be trained to *logically* defend the Word of God:

> But sanctify the Lord God in your hearts: and be ready always to give an answer to every man that asketh you a reason of the hope that is in you with meekness and fear (1 Pet. 3:15).

> CHURCHES HAVEN'T TRAINED THEIR PEOPLE TO DEFEND THE BIBLE AGAINST THE ONSLAUGHTS OF EVOLUTIONARY HUMANISM; INSTEAD THEY'VE BEEN *INFLUENCED* BY IT.

Churches haven't trained their people to defend the Bible against the onslaughts of evolutionary humanism; instead they've been *influenced* by it. If a skeptic were to approach the average Christian today and ask questions like: Where did the Bible come from? How do you know it's the Word of God? Where did God come from? How did Noah get all the animals on the ark? How do you fit dinosaurs with the Bible? If we all go back to Adam and Eve, where did Cain get his wife?

I suggest that most Christians would not have answers to these and many other basic questions.

These are just some of the questions that are thrown at Christians today to intimidate them, because the humanists know most Christians can't answer them. God's people have been so evolutionized that they just ignore these questions and tell people to just trust in Jesus. But these are the questions that need to be answered to show we can defend God's Word. When this happens, it actually opens the door to talking more about the Bible and presenting the salvation message.

When my brother was in seminary, a Christian worker in the school system came to speak to the students about evangelism in public schools. During his lecture, he told these seminary students that the two most-asked questions he received were, "Where did Cain get his wife?" and "What about evolution?" He then laughed and told the students to ignore these questions, that they were just "red herrings."

Wrong. They are *not* red herrings. The reason these are the two most-asked questions is because they illustrate the real foundational problem. The school students are really challenging Christianity: "Come up with answers — we know you can't. Why should we believe the Bible when you can't answer these questions? We know evolution's true — science has proved the Bible wrong. You believe in Adam and Eve, well, you can't; you don't know where Cain's wife came from, so we're not interested in Christianity."

So where does this leave us? What's the solution? There is a solution, but only if we are prepared to put on the correct pair of glasses!

Last year, you came to Louisville and I attended one of your seminars. Your ministry has been an answer to my prayers. I grew up in an alcoholic home in which God was not a part. In public schools, I was taught evolution. Even as a lost sinner, evolution made no sense. I often thought, *I did not come from a monkey.* Creation spoke to my heart that there was a Creator.

After I married, I came to know the Lord. After becoming a Christian, I still heard pastors using the "thousand years as one day" Scripture to fit creation into an evolutionary box. This left me confused. I rejoice that the Lord led me to your ministry. I am learning to trust in God's Word. Thank you for coming to Louisville and for sharing.

T.L., Kentucky

CHAPTER 9

BEAUTY AND THE CURSE

T he well-known hymn "All Things Bright and Beautiful" is sung widely in churches. Even though this is a wonderful hymn, and I enjoy singing it, in some ways it actually portrays the world incorrectly.

If you were to come with me to the tropical rainforests of the deep north in Australia, we might encounter a deadly stinging tree. If you were to just brush up against the leaves of this tree, you would receive a painful sting that can last for years. Imagine you were just stung by this tree. So in great pain you rush down the hillside to the nearby ocean to wash your arm. Immediately you get stung by one of Australia's deadly tropical sea stingers (you could die in minutes). You crawl out of the ocean, and fall into a nearby freshwater creek, and just as you are being taken into the jaws of a man-eating crocodile, you begin singing that hymn —"All Things Bright And Beautiful."

In the real world, all things are not that beautiful, are they? Sometimes I think we should have an extra verse to that hymn that goes like this: "All things marred and mutated — the Lord God *cursed* them all."

When Christians look at the world, it needs to be understood that they are looking at a fallen world. This is not the world God made, but it's the world He made and then cursed because of sin. It is a groaning world given over to futility (Rom. 8:22).

This observation is so important because most Christians today don't communicate real Christianity to non-Christians because of the foundational change discussed in the last chapter.

Consider this illustration: Imagine you, as a Christian, were to take a non-Christian to the Grand Canyon. I've been there — it's a magnificent place. The views are indescribable. As you stand on the edge of this mile-deep canyon, you say to your non-Christian friend, "Look at all this beauty. Can't you see there's a God of love? It's such a beautiful world."

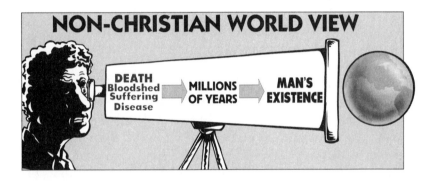

NON-CHRISTIAN WORLD VIEW

DEATH Bloodshed Suffering Disease → MILLIONS OF YEARS → MAN'S EXISTENCE

Your non-Christian friend looks at you and responds: "What are you talking about? All I see are billions of dead things buried in rock layers, laid down by water all over the area. The layers of this canyon are full of dead things (fossils) representing millions of years of death, disease, and struggle. Around the world I see children dying, people starving, senseless killings, terrorism, horrible accidents. I don't see a beautiful world. I see physical and emotional pain everywhere I look. It's a chaotic world. It's a world where only the fit survive — the weak get stomped on. I don't see a God of order and love. If He does exist, He must be a vicious and hateful God."

The problem is that you and your friend are looking at the canyon (and the world) through different eyes. If you put on truly biblical glasses, and look at the world through the Bible, then we know that God created a perfect world, but man rebelled. Sin entered the world, and thus death and the Curse came as a consequence of the judgment of a Holy God. And look what *our* sin has done to this world: children abused, families splitting apart, mental diseases, rapes, cancer killing our loved ones, etc. It's a horrible world. But a Christian understands there's a God of love because even though man rebelled, God sent His Son to die so we can be restored to our Creator.

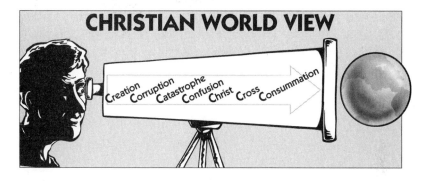

Sadly, even most Christians don't have the correct glasses on. They've been indoctrinated to believe in millions of years of death and suffering before man. Even though they believe in a God of love, they can't respond adequately to the questions of the non-Christian. It's only when a Christian understands the origin of death and suffering because of Adam's fall that they will be able to give answers.

Because most of the Church has accepted the teaching that there were millions of years of death and suffering before Adam, they don't have the answers! But the Word of God *has* — if only the Church would realize it.

And because the non-Christian has been indoctrinated to believe in millions of years of death, suffering, disease, and blood-shed, he doesn't understand how there can be a God of love. This person is not going to understand about a God of love until he puts on the true, uncompromised, biblical glasses, including the time-line of history: from creation, through the Fall, the Cross and Resurrection and the final consummation of all these. Also, until the Christian has put on these same glasses, he will not be able to explain this seemingly contradictory world of death and life, health and disease, and joy and suffering to the non-Christian.

These Christians will probably never understand the believer's hope of a future state that will again be perfect just as it was before sin. How can there be a restoration to such a perfect state when there never was one to start with? Thus, they don't long for heaven. They are "content" with a grim outlook on life and don't really have a clue about real joy. This leads to Christians becoming spiritually bankrupt and lukewarm. They become apathetic — they don't understand the gospel and what it means. No wonder Christianity seems to have lost its power. It's because Christians have lost *real* Christianity, which is based on the *Word* of the living God.

Again, both the non-Christian and the Christian are thinking like "Greeks." They need to begin thinking like "Jews" before they can fully comprehend the message of God's love.

Let us now consider the solution. Carefully observe the following castle diagram labeled "The Solution."

This is basically the same castle as the previous one, except this time notice that the Christians have aimed their guns at the foundation of the humanist castle, as well as at their weapons, *and* at the issues. At the same time, Christians are rebuilding the foundation of God's Word.

What I am saying again is this: issues such as abortion are just symptoms of the foundational change. Thus, one can't change the culture back to a Christian philosophy just by attacking the issues. Christian morality can't ultimately and consistently stand on the wrong foundation of evolution. If the approach is merely to try to get politicians to change the laws about abortion, homosexual behavior, and the like, it won't work in the long run. Even if some laws were changed to be more consistent with Christian thinking, what happens if new legislators who don't accept Christianity get voted in? They'll just change the laws back again.

You can't change a system from the top down when it has changed from the foundation up. Fighting the issues may bring these things to people's attention. And it may stimulate much discussion and debate. But in the long run, this approach will not change society. What is the solution? The Great Commission and many other passages tell me to preach the authority of the Word of God — to preach the gospel and see people saved. If someone truly is born again and builds his thinking on God's Word and develops a truly Christian way of thinking, then he will apply this thinking in the culture. The more people do this, the more the culture will change. Surely this is part of being the Bible's "salt" and "light" in this world.

Notice that on the diagram, I show the Christians doing four things:

1. Rebuilding the foundation of God's Word. Christians need to accept the authority of the Word of God beginning with Genesis. It's vital that they reject the compromise so many Christians have with evolutionary ideas. The Church can't even begin to bring about a foundational change back to the Word of God until they believe all of the Word of God.

As a part of this, the Church also needs to be teaching people how to defend the Bible, how to answer the questions of the skeptics, and how to present positive solutions to contemporary issues that are used to undermine the Bible.

God's people need to understand Christian doctrines and their foundations in Genesis. They need to know how to build these doctrines in their lives and the lives of their children.[1]

2. Christians attacking humanism at its foundation. They need to understand that evolution is an anti-God religion. They should become familiar with the simple arguments of science that can easily refute evolutionary teaching.[2]

3. Christians fighting the weapons that are being used against them. They need to come up with programs to counteract the education system, television programs, magazines, and other means used to disseminate evolutionary propaganda.[3]

4. Christians standing against the evils of abortion, homosexual behavior, pornography, and the other such ills that plague our society. But we should stand against them knowing how to defend our position. We shouldn't be seen just to be against them because we think they're wrong. We need to think foundationally and know why these issues are wrong, and *why* non-Christians don't understand why we think this way.[4]

In summary then: First, it's vital for the Church to understand that the culture as a whole has changed foundationally from being like the "Jews" to being like the "Greeks." Evangelistic methods must take this into account, or they will become increasingly ineffective.

Second, the Church itself needs to recognize that it has become like the "Greeks." This is why the Church hasn't understood the foundational change in the culture. And this is why many Christians aren't successful in reaching today's people with the gospel.

Now some might say, "But I attend a church where we have a great outreach program. We see people being won to the Lord each week. Admittedly we are not talking about large numbers, but our evangelism program works." I agree that this does occur in many churches. However, we need to understand that there still is quite a remnant of Christian influence in many of our Western nations. In America, for instance, there are still millions of non-Christians who have some vestige of Christian influence in their background.

But at the same time, we must look ahead and understand that this Christian basis is slowly disappearing. Years ago, there was much plowed ground — plowed by the churches and even the schools.

The enemy, however, has sown seeds of destruction. Much of the plowed ground is now covered with the trees of evolutionary biology and the rocks of evolutionary geology. Although there is still some plowed ground, it is disappearing at an alarming rate. Many of the younger generations are coming through an education system that has trained them in an anti-Christian philosophy.

In a sense, I picture the "creation evangelist" as one who is using a bulldozer to plow the ground, first to rid it of rocks, trees, and debris that have prevented the seed from taking root. Evolution is one of the biggest, if not *the* biggest, stumbling block to people listening to the gospel today. This stumbling block must be removed. The enemy has taken over the territory, and we need to claim it back. Plowing the ground and preparing the foundation — that's what "creation evangelism" is all about.

99

Even though evangelistic efforts still reap some harvest, I suggest that it's not what it was generations ago. In most instances today it is not the harvest of Acts 2.

Now, I'm not saying that pioneer evangelism (or pre-evangelism or "creation evangelism") is the only method of evangelism. There are many methods. In the Bible we see that the apostles and Jesus Christ used different methods to reach different people. And that's the point. We need to understand people's biases. We shouldn't be using just one method of evangelism. Creation evangelism is not the only method in the tool box, but it is one that must be a predominant tool for today's "Greek" culture. I believe that pioneering evangelism needs to be adopted on a large scale (as part of a church's normal evangelistic approach) if we are going to continue to reach people with the gospel.

To put it another way, the ground Peter was working with (in Acts 2) was soft ground (i.e., prepared soil, ready to be planted). However, in Acts 17, Paul encountered much harder ground. Today, I believe the ground is harder than it was in Paul's day: not only are people lacking the foundational knowledge of the Bible and Christianity, but because this is actively taught *against*, it is much more difficult to get people to respond to the truth of God's Word. I was reminded of this when a missionary to an isolated Indian tribe in Mexico visited our church in San Diego. He felt it was easier to reach this Indian tribe with the gospel than university students in California, saying, "At least the Indians still believe in God."

Today there is also a lot of "bad" Christianity. Compromise is rife throughout the Church. In a real sense, this culture would be easier to approach with the gospel if it was totally pagan.

Creation evangelism, though, works to overcome these very difficult circumstances — which shouldn't be surprising, for it was given to us in the Book of Acts as a pattern to follow. A selection of testimonies from our files is given in chapter 14 to substantiate this.

If we don't start reclaiming the ground Christianity has lost, then in generations to come there may be no plowed ground remaining. We must also recognize that there is no quick-fix solution to combat more than a century of evolutionary indoctrination.

Remember when the armies of a number of countries went to Kuwait to reclaim the ground taken over by the enemy? The United States "drew a line in the sand." In a similar way, there is a spiritual battle taking place in our culture today when we attempt to retrieve ground from the enemy (Satan).

Isn't it interesting to note how emotional the creation/evolution issue has become? You can talk about all sorts of topics in public schools, but as soon as you mention creation/evolution, there is an almost instant reaction. This is because the humanists know where the real battle is being waged. There is no more foundational message than God is Creator. After all, if God is not Creator, then nothing else matters. All is meaningless.

The fact that the creation/evolution issue evokes such emotional and vocal responses should speak loudly to the Church that this is the real front line of the battle between humanism and Christianity. It even creates division among Christians because many have compromised with millions of years of history or other aspects of evolutionary philosophy. Some claim that we should only teach things that unite, not divide.

After I had spoken at a Christian college, some of the students informed me that on the day before, one of the professors had tried to pre-empt my lecture by informing the students that creation ministries are divisive — the implication being that those who accept a literal Genesis are divisive, but those who insist on other positions are not divisive.

The Creator of the world, the Lord Jesus Christ, during His earthly ministry, brought division: "Think not that I am come to send peace on earth: I came not to send peace, but a sword. For I am come to set a man at variance against his father, and the daughter against her mother, and the daughter-in-law against her mother-in-law" (Matt. 10:34–35). In Luke 12:51 we read, "Suppose ye that I am come to give peace on earth? I tell you, Nay; but rather division."

And what happened as a result of Christ's ministry? "So there was a division among the people because of him" (John 7:43). "There was a division therefore again among the Jews for these sayings" (John 10:19). I am sure that some of the religious leaders of the day accused Christ of being divisive.

The point is that the truth *is* divisive! Because Christ is the truth, His ministry was divisive. Because the Answers in Genesis ministry insists on the literal truth of Genesis (God's Word), then those Christians who have compromised with evolutionary ideas and/or millions of years call us divisive.

Many people think that people like myself are biased and thus divisive, but that others are just neutral. However, it is important to understand that God's Word tells us there is no such thing as neutrality. We are told that we either walk in light or in darkness — there is no in-between. In Matthew 12:30, we read, "He that is not with me is against me: and he that gathereth not with me scattereth abroad."

Those who compromise the Bible to fit evolution/long-age philosophy often exhibit what my friend Carl Wieland calls "the herd mentality," the desire to win approval from the world: "The herd says Genesis is to be taken as myth or allegory."

I remember an incident in England after speaking to a prestigious Christian group on the campus of Cambridge University. During my lecture on the importance of Genesis, a young man jumped up and blurted out, "But you're coming across as if what you're saying is true!"

I replied, "I wouldn't be saying these things if I didn't believe them!"

I spent time with this young man discussing the problem he had with what I was saying. He wanted me to allow for other opinions, and not just sound as though what I was saying had to be the truth. He accused me of being narrow-minded and biased, while he claimed to be open-minded, allowing for other opinions.

When I asked him if he was "open-minded" enough to allow for my opinion, which dictated that Genesis had to be taken literally, he realized we had reached an impasse. He was insisting that I allow for the possibility that my position was not correct, and that other opinions should be put on the same level. I asked if he were open-minded enough to allow for my position, which stated that all other positions were wrong! My position was intolerant of his — but his position was also intolerant of mine!

This reminds me of Christian colleges whose spokespersons state that they allow all views on Genesis. However, they refuse to permit the view that only those who take Genesis literally have the correct view! Such colleges, like the opinion of the student above, have taken a dogmatic stand that does not allow for the position that one must take Genesis literally (at face value) and that all other positions are wrong.

As long as the creationist ministry exists in this world, it *will* be divisive. The truth always is! When we shine light in a dark world, division must occur.

One should not judge a method or message on the basis of whether it is divisive or not, but on the basis of whether it is truth and based on the Bible. Creation evangelism, as divisive as it is, is a light shining in a world of darkness. Christians need to come to grips with this and begin using this powerful method of reaching people with the gospel.

> ONE SHOULD NOT JUDGE A METHOD OR MESSAGE ON THE BASIS OF WHETHER IT IS DIVISIVE OR NOT, BUT ON THE BASIS OF WHETHER IT IS TRUTH AND BASED ON THE BIBLE.

I've actually had some Christians say to me, "Okay, even if what you're saying is true, what you are advocating takes a lot of time and work. The Lord may come back anytime. We just need to get people saved. There's no point spending years dealing with this foundational problem. If it's taken years for this foundation to change, it could take years to change it back. In the meantime, millions of souls could be lost. No, we need to just get people saved, even if they don't understand Christianity totally. It's more important to get them into heaven."

I recall a conversation I once had with Dr. Henry Morris, from the Institute for Creation Research. Dr. Morris was giving me some background on the book *The Genesis Flood,* authored by Dr. Morris and Dr. John Whitcomb. This is the book that greatly stimulated the formation of creation ministries worldwide.

I remember Dr. Morris telling me that he nearly did not write this book, as he thought it was more important to preach the gospel and see people saved. He recognized that the emphasis of this book in counteracting evolutionary philosophy and restoring the biblical foundation was a really long-term vision. To change a whole way of thinking in the Church takes such a long time. Surely, he reasoned, the Lord will come back soon — maybe we should just preach the gospel.

As a result of Drs. Morris and Whitcomb's book, written over 30 years ago, creation organizations have formed around the world, and millions have now heard the gospel through them. *The Genesis Flood* was, in reality, a creation evangelism thrust. What a mighty work this has been in seeing people fired up for the Lord and souls won!

When I think back to the time when my wife, Mally, and I made the decision for me to leave teaching and begin a full-time creation ministry in 1979, I never realized then the real power of creation evangelism. In fact, when one considered the inroads evolutionary teaching had made in the education system, and society in general, it seemed an impossible task for a small group of people to combat this seemingly invincible giant. But the Lord blesses those who stand uncompromisingly on His infallible Word. The Lord has used this ministry to win many souls and fire up Christians to be involved in this battle for souls.

From a biblical perspective, and recognizing God's sovereignty, we know that not one of the souls given to the Son by the Father will be lost (John 17).

From our perspective of human responsibility, we are to do our best to reach the lost. And here is where I have a big problem with the claim that we just need to get people saved. I've seen some research studies that indicate that the divorce rate among people who call themselves born-again Christians is higher than that in the world.[5] The abortion rate is also very high in the Church.

Personally I believe there has been so much "easy believism" (i.e., just trust in Jesus) in churches and evangelistic thrusts that our churches are full of people who have added Jesus in with all their other "gods." People can easily have an emotional experience, and decide to trust Jesus, but if they don't know what that means — if they haven't had true repentance, for instance — then are they truly converted?

Let's be honest. Many times these people have not properly understood their sin. Perhaps, they came forward in a last-ditch effort to escape from their pain. They never had a clear understanding of their sin. After saying a prayer, they go on to live just as they lived before! For truly effective evangelism and dedicated discipleship, we must use "creation evangelism" so they understand sin and the need for repentance. Then they also need discipling to understand what it really means to be a Christian and have a Christian world view.

Let me illustrate this with a practical example. New Tribes Mission is a missionary organization that has documented an enormous problem they faced in their efforts to reach pagan tribes.[6]

Like most other missionary organizations, their missionaries concentrated on the New Testament when teaching native people about Christ. They called for commitments, and thought many were converted. As time went on, they realized that there weren't many sincere conversions at all. Eventually, New Tribes changed its method of approach. They started teaching the Christian message from the beginnings in Genesis. They realized that these tribal people had no Christian basis at all. So how would they really understand sin, and why Jesus died?

New Tribes developed a chronological teaching curriculum that enabled the missionaries to teach from creation to Christ.[7] They started at the beginning!

It is really such a simple concept. One can't fully understand what happened on the Cross until there is an understanding of the history in the Old Testament (the significance of the Passover lamb, for instance).

New Tribes found that after laying this foundation, when they did get to the message of the Cross, the response was overwhelming. The commitments to Christ were many and sincere.[8]

When we read a book or watch a movie, we don't skip the first half and then read or watch the rest. We start at the beginning so we will understand the story line correctly. Why is it, though, that most Christians, when they read the Bible, start toward the end?

I remember one lady in a church who came up to me and very excitedly told me what my message had done for her that morning. She said, "I have been a Christian for two years. I was told to study the Book of John. But I just didn't really understand what Christianity was all about. After your sermon on Genesis, I feel as if a light bulb has suddenly gone on in my head. Because you took me back to the beginning, now I understand the plot. For the first time I am understanding what Christianity is all about. *No one ever suggested I start reading the Bible at the beginning."*

And here is another practical suggestion for evangelism today. Many times, we hand out the New Testament, perhaps with the Psalms and Proverbs, as well. However, without the Old Testament, and particularly the Book of Genesis, there is no foundation for the New Testament. People who have been taught evolution will not be able see the true account of the history of the universe and life to understand that what they believe is wrong. At the very least today, we need to ensure that people get the first 11 chapters of Genesis along with the New Testament.

In fact, I've often thought that a good tract to hand out would be the passages of Genesis 1–11, Exodus 20 (the Law), John, Romans, 1 Corinthians 15, and Revelation 21–22. In a sense, these excerpts from the Bible would give someone a complete understanding of the foundation, power, and hope of the gospel.

REACHING PAGAN TRIBES WITH CREATION EVANGELISM

There is another vital aspect of creation evangelism: it is also a powerful method for reaching pagan tribes.

I think many mission organizations have not understood the underlying reason why certain peoples have responded positively to the gospel, and thus these missions have failed to capitalize on a powerful way to teach God's Word.

Years ago I was visiting an aboriginal mission station in Australia. Because of my background in the creation ministry,

I knew that most cultures around the world (American Indians, Fijians, Eskimos, Hawaiians, and the Australian Aborigines for example) had legends handed down from their ancestors that sounded like the Noah's flood account and other accounts in Genesis. This to me, of course, was evidence that these cultures had all descended from Noah and had handed down these stories based originally on the true accounts, but changed them somewhat over the years.

The missionary was explaining to me how difficult it was to reach the aboriginal culture with the gospel. I asked him whether he had heard of dreamtime legends about a flood or a creation account. He thought for a while, and then started telling me some of the stories the Aborigines say were handed down for generations. As we spoke, the missionary said he'd often thought about why these legends sounded so similar to the creation/flood account in Genesis. But he had never really put it together. His missionary organization knew of such stories, but never suggested they be used as part of their evangelism.

I pointed out to him that this could be a real starting point for presenting the truth of God's Word. After all, these people had similar stories to the Bible.

A couple of years later, I met this missionary again. He related a fascinating story. One day he was sitting down with an aboriginal elder. This old man told the missionary that the Aborigines believed that the first woman was made while the first man was asleep. The missionary then read the account of the creation of Eve from Genesis. The Aborigine looked shocked and asked, "How come you have the same story we have? And your story is better." Sometime later, this missionary led this Aborigine to the Lord Jesus Christ!

Don Richardson, in his well-known and classic work *Eternity in Their Hearts,* gives many examples of people who had been unreached with Christianity, yet responded to the gospel because there was enough knowledge of the true God still retained in their culture.[9] He writes that the greatest missionary successes have come when missionaries identified the Creator God in the people's own legends with the true God of the Bible.

Yet, most missionaries and missionary organizations have neglected this approach. Richardson comments in his book, "Followers of Christ around the world and down through the centuries could have had 100 times more missionary vigor if seminary professors, pastors, and church school teachers had understood and communicated this central theme as the Bible communicates it."[10]

And then there are countries in which missionaries work in societies with religions that deny the existence of one holy transcendent Creator and are evolutionary in their beliefs. For example, they begin with a belief in pre-existing matter.

These people, too, need a creation evangelism approach. Missionaries need to counteract their evolutionary views and establish the right foundation for the structure of the gospel. I believe that one of the major reasons that missionaries have not used a creation evangelism approach is because they have been so influenced by evolution or millions of years that they don't see Genesis as essential or useful in evangelism. Thus, they don't see the importance of such a method. They have missed the foundational problem. They still have this idea that the only way to present the gospel is to preach the New Testament message of sin, repentance, and trust in Jesus Christ.

> UNTIL THE CHURCH GETS ITS FOUNDATION RIGHT, IT IS NOT GOING TO MAKE A SIGNIFICANT IMPACT ON THE CULTURE, REGARDLESS OF HOW SUCCESSFUL PROGRAMS ARE IN ATTRACTING PEOPLE.

Even within creation evangelism itself, there are different approaches depending on the particular background of the people being reached.

Another important point to note about Paul's pioneer evangelism is that when ministering to "Greeks," one wouldn't expect them to come to where the "Jews" were. Paul didn't invite the Greek philosophers to a service in the local synagogue — he didn't start his meeting with them in a word of prayer, or hand out song sheets to sing hymns. Paul

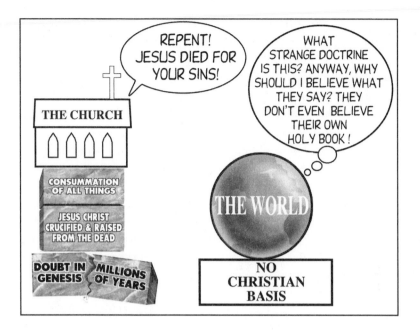

met them "where they were." He even used quotes from their own poets and playwrights. At the same time, he didn't water down the teaching of the Word. Instead, he used a method of teaching to get them to the point of understanding the Word of God. Their church attendance would come later.

Today, many churches in our Western world have recognized that they are not reaching the world. They try to bridge the gap between the Church and the world by emphasizing entertainment programs with which the world would be familiar. Thus, the emphasis is on getting people in so that they will "enjoy themselves." In most instances, this only results in a "watering down" of the teaching of the Word.

Even many seminaries and Bible colleges are recommending this entertainment approach. Rarely do we see pastors and church leaders today who are trained in teaching God's Word verse by verse and applying it in the culture. Expository preaching is becoming a lost art.

Of course, many of these church leaders and seminary professors would claim that we are ministering to a different culture.

Their needs are different. I agree, but not in the way these leaders understand. They are not thinking in terms of "Greeks" rather than "Jews." They are thinking more in terms of this being a technology-driven culture — people are influenced by television and are not as interested in spiritual things. Materialism is their God. But most of the Church is missing the *foundational* reason for this culture's philosophy.

Until the Church gets its foundation right, it is not going to make a significant impact on the culture, regardless of how successful programs are in attracting people.

Compounding this problem is the fact that to many Christians, numbers are a measure of success. However, people living consistent Christian lives, being salt and light, separated from the world (but in it and influencing it), should be the measure of success. This will, in the long run, also lead to greater numbers of true converts.

Some of the "mega churches" may attract large crowds with their extravagant programs. Yes, some people may even be saved, but in the end, if the correct foundation has not been laid, it will amount to very little.

So where should we start? If what I'm saying is correct, it seems to be an almost overwhelming task. Where can we begin to turn the tide?

I became a Christian several years ago, but I still held on to the possibility of an old earth. That's when I wrote a critical letter to you. Your staff responded with a letter and as a result of that and the tape *Challenge to the Church,* I reversed my position. I completely understand now how fallible scientific theories of dating and origins undermine Genesis and ultimately destroy the meaning of the Cross. Keep up the good work.

D.J., Kentucky

CHAPTER **10**

THE SEVEN CS

W hen I first visited America in the early eighties, I was asked to be a guest on a number of talk show programs on Christian radio. At first I was rather nervous about what questions I would be asked. As time went on, however, I found out that I was asked the same questions that people in Australian churches would also ask me. Let me summarize them for you:

> Where did Cain get his wife?
> Can't Christians believe in evolution?
> Doesn't carbon dating prove the earth is very old?
> How do dinosaurs fit with the Bible?
> Haven't scientists proved the earth is billions of years old?
> How did Noah get all the animals on the ark?
> Wasn't there a gap between the first two verses in Genesis?
> Isn't a day like a thousand years, so the days of creation must be long periods?
> Where did all the different "races" of people come from?
> How do you explain the "ape-men"?
> Are the days of creation ordinary days?

In 1987 we moved to the United States. Since that time I have appeared on numerous radio talk shows. You know what is fascinating? I basically get the same questions from listeners every time! Sometimes, a talk show host will ask me before we go on the air about what sort of questions I think the callers will ask.

My standard reply is this: "Well, let me tell you. . . ." And I run down the above list.

What I've tried to do over the years is to incorporate the answers to these questions into my talks, knowing that most people in the audience, by and large, want answers to these. This situation stimulated us to produce a book called *The New Answers Book*[1] that offers detailed answers to these most-asked questions.

Now this experience tells me something very important. The average Christian obviously is not getting the answers to these questions from their churches or Christian schools.

And then I found out something even more interesting. Back in 1925 at the famous Scopes trial in Dayton, Tennessee, William Jennings Bryan, the man who really represented Christianity at the trial, was asked some of these same questions.[2] He could not answer them![3] Sadly, nothing much seems to have changed since then.

I'm even asked many of these same questions when I appear on secular talk shows. I believe this is because there are people in the secular world who know that most Christians can't answer them, particularly questions like "Where did Cain get his wife?" Thus, to the non-Christian, the fact that Christians don't have answers is their justification for not believing the Bible.

Also, I've found that Christians from conservative Bible-believing churches ask many of the same questions. *Again, I believe that most Christians can't connect the Bible with the real world because they've been so influenced by the world's teachings.* Even if they don't believe in evolution per se, they still have been indoctrinated in millions of years of history and other evolutionary teaching. The attacks on Genesis have been so massive that most Christians have given up trying to defend it. Now they can't answer basic questions. And if they can't answer these questions, then their children won't be able to either. Thus, their children could easily reject all of the Bible, which is what has been happening at an alarming rate in Christianity.

Most people in our churches don't understand that the Bible is a history book. Christianity is not based on myth or interesting stories — it is based on real history. There was a real Adam, to whom we are all related. There was a real Garden and Fall, which is why we are all sinners. There was a real Curse, which is why there is death and suffering.

A pastor might be the best Bible expositor in the world. He may be teaching his people verse by verse through Scripture (which, by the way, is the type of Bible teaching we all need). Nonetheless, if most of the congregation can't answer the questions above — and even if this pastor expounds every verse in Genesis correctly — he will still not reach his people. If pastors can't connect it to the *real* world, then it's almost "pie in the sky." I find that many Christians look on the Bible only as a book about salvation. To them, Christianity is only about getting saved, going to heaven, and warning people about hell.

> FROM WHAT DO WE NEED TO BE SAVED IF THE BIBLE REALLY CAN'T BE TRUSTED?

But Christianity is *much* more than this. It is a whole way of thinking and living in today's world. When our children ask questions about the *real* world — questions like the above, concerning dinosaurs, fossils, Noah's ark, Cain's wife, and races — we need to show them that the Bible connects *all* this to reality. If the connection to real history is lost, then ultimately what does it mean to be saved? From what do we need to be saved if the Bible really can't be trusted?

After I spoke at one church, a man came up to me and said, "Wow, I didn't realize how important Genesis is. I've never thought about that. I'm excited. Where are those books you mentioned — I want to buy some."

The pastor standing nearby came and said to me, "I don't understand. I've preached my heart out on Genesis and this man just argued with me for months. You come in here and give one talk, and he's turned around. What happened?"

What happened was that I explained Genesis not just from the text, but connected it to the real world, pointing out the inconsistencies of believing what the world was teaching — and answering some of the most-asked questions I knew people like this man would have.

It's a very different way of teaching Genesis.

To illustrate this further, let me share with you the philosophy behind a Bible curriculum we are preparing. I believe this way of teaching should be applied in *all* of our Bible teaching in the Church anyway.

We call it the "Seven Cs" approach. The Seven Cs represent major events in history from the Bible. We start at the beginning, and follow a time-line of history to its end.

Creation
Corruption
Catastrophe
Confusion
Christ
Cross
Consummation

Now, of course, there are many other events one could add, but these are some of the major events of history. We put them on a time-line from the beginning (about 6,000 years ago) up until the present, then on into the future. When you think about it, *everything* we teach in Christianity goes back to this time-line of history. And this is the point: we need to show people that the Bible is a *history book*, and that everything connects to *real* history.

As we teach through the Bible, then, I believe we always need to incorporate *four* major thrusts.

The Seven C's of History

Creation Corruption Catastrophe Confusion Christ Cross Consummation

1. We need to clearly teach—from the plain language—what the Bible states. For instance, because it is God's Word (and not *just* a human work), then Scripture must be self-authenticating and self-attesting, and Scripture must interpret Scripture. Certainly, extra-biblical sources can be used to aid us in understanding the background against which it was written, but these sources must be secondary to the context of the Bible's words themselves.

2. Because the world is against the Bible, we must be certain that we understand what the world is saying and doing in attacking and undermining the Bible. This must then be counteracted.

3. Christians should be taught how to logically defend what the Bible is teaching us, taking into account how the secular world (and even other Christians) attack this point. Because many Christians have compromised with the world's teachings, people need to be taught why these compromise positions are wrong, so they can defend their faith to other believers. This overlaps with point 4.

4. The doctrine that comes out of this section needs to be clearly enunciated and then application made to our daily living.

Let's get specific with some practical examples.

A. WE ARE TEACHING ABOUT THE CREATION OF ADAM AND EVE:

And the Lord God formed man of the dust of the ground, and breathed into his nostrils the breath of life; and man became a living soul (Gen. 2:7).

And the Lord God caused a deep sleep to fall upon Adam, and he slept: and he took one of his ribs, and closed up the flesh instead thereof; And the rib, which the Lord God had taken from man, made he a woman, and brought her unto the man. And Adam said, This is now bone of my bones, and flesh of my flesh: she shall be called Woman, because she was taken out of Man. Therefore shall a man leave his father and his mother, and shall cleave unto his wife: and they shall be one flesh (Gen. 2:21–24).

1. The Bible clearly states that Adam was made from dust and Eve from his side.

115

2. The world, however, teaches that man evolved from an "ape-man" and woman from an "ape-woman." This teaching needs to be shown as wrong. Examples of so-called "ape-men" could be refuted.

3. Christians can be taught how to defend that there was one man and one woman at the beginning. Passages of Scripture such as 1 Corinthians 15:45 and Genesis 3:20 could be used. Scientific evidence of the close genetic relatedness of all people can be shown not as "proof," but as solid evidence.[4]

4. The doctrine of marriage — one man for one woman for life — should be explained. The fact that we become one in marriage (see Matt. 19:4–6 and Eph. 5:28–29), because Eve was taken out of Adam — they were one flesh. Eve could not have come from some pre-existing animal — this would destroy the basis of oneness in marriage.

B. THE TEACHING OF THE FALL OF ADAM:

1. The Bible clearly states there was a literal tree, garden, serpent, temptation, fruit, and Adam. Adam literally rebelled. Sin entered the world — and it had consequences.

2. The world, however, teaches that there was no such event in history. The world talks about the doctrine of uniformitarianism — the belief that things have basically gone on as they are for millions of years. Christians could bring up events in geology (such as the eruption of Mount St. Helens[5]) and their consequences (rapid sedimentary layering, canyon formation, etc.) that could be used to refute this. Because death, disease, bloodshed, and suffering were a consequence of sin, one can't have millions of years of death and disease in a fossil record before Adam.

3. Christians need to be able to defend that there had to be a literal Fall — that this explains the origin of death and suffering. This is the only thing that explains a seemingly contradictory world. The Fall has to be a literal event in history or sin cannot be defined. Christians have to believe in this account as literal history.

4. The doctrine of sin, its consequences, and the fact that we are all descendants of this first man is why we are sinners — and why we need salvation. And there is the doctrine of the restoration, the future removal of the Curse.

C. THE CROSS AND RESURRECTION:

1. The Bible clearly teaches the death and resurrection of Jesus Christ. It was a literal resurrection.

2. The world, however, says that Jesus was just a man — so this needs to be counteracted by Christians. Some say Jesus really didn't rise from the dead — the so-called "swoon theory." There are many fine books that help us defend the historicity of this account.

3. People need to be taught that the reason He died was because death was the penalty for sin. That's why Christians can't believe in millions of years of history and add it to the Bible.[6]

4. The doctrine of the Resurrection is central to the gospel. Jesus is called the "last Adam" for He became the new head of the human race, taking the place of the "first Adam."[7]

Whenever Bible teachers are expounding the Word of God, they should always keep in mind that what they are teaching is attacked from within and without the Church. By teaching their people how to defend the Bible against those attacks, Bible teachers will equip Christians to be much more prepared to defend the Bible in public and to teach their children authoritatively.

One of the reasons I emphasize this is because it was so true in my own life. My father always was one to defend the Bible against the attacks of the day. It wasn't good enough for him just to say "Believe it and don't worry about what others say." He saw the necessity to logically defend the Bible — knowing, of course, that it does stand on its own anyway.

When it came to times when my father didn't have answers, he didn't capitulate to what others were saying. He would patiently research the answers. For instance, when I asked my father about the evolutionary teaching I was receiving at school, he didn't have any answers at first. We didn't have the wealth of materials we have today. But instead of doing what many Christians did (e.g., tell their children they could add evolution to the Bible, or that it didn't matter), he pointed out the importance of believing in a literal Genesis. As far as the science was concerned, he said we would have to wait. For him, if he was sure the Bible text taught something clearly, he would stick by this regardless. This greatly influenced me. When the answers did come, he was excited that he could now counteract what the world was teaching.

When I have visited youth groups, Christian schools, and other church groups over the years, I've been so disappointed to find that although many might be on fire for the Lord, most of them could not answer basic questions about Christianity. They couldn't really defend their faith.

Young people coming out of a Christian school or college can have the best results academically, leave with undergraduate and graduate degrees, and get prestigious jobs — but if they can't defend their faith and effectively proclaim the gospel in an increasingly secular society, what good is all that education?

Here are just some of the basic questions that many Christians can't answer. Why not seriously think about whether you (or the people in your church) can answer these adequately:

> Where did the Bible come from? Why is it the Word of God? How do we know it's infallible? Who wrote the Bible? Why is Christianity better than Buddhism? How do we know there's a God? Where did God come from?

When you think about it, these are really very basic questions. And of course there are these:

> Where did Cain get his wife? Can't Christians believe in evolution? Doesn't carbon dating prove the earth to be very old? How do dinosaurs fit with the Bible? Haven't scientists proved the earth is billions of years old? How did Noah get all the animals on the ark? Wasn't there a gap between the first two verses in Genesis? Isn't a day like a thousand years, so the days of creation must be long periods? Where did all the different "races" of people come from? How do you explain the "ape-men"? Are the days of creation ordinary days?

I believe that much of the Church is in a rut. We almost need to stop what we are doing and go back to the very basics.

Teachers need to be instructing people on how to defend the very basics of Christianity. This is where I see the modern Church failing in a big way. There is too much emotionalism — too many programs — and not enough teaching of the Word and how to defend it in today's world. There is very little understanding of the real foundational problem that has led to our moral crisis in society. This lack of understanding of the basic problem is also seen in the way the Church generally views the doctrine of creation.

Over the years, I have heard many Christians argue that a ministry like Answers in Genesis is not that important because creation, after all, is only a "secondary doctrine." They believe it is much more important to concentrate on the New Testament and its teachings concerning Christ.

For instance, one of our supporters wrote to the founder and president of Promise Keepers (Bill McCartney), asking about Promise Keepers' stand on the creation issue. The response received from the assistant to the president reflects what I believe is much of the Church's attitude to this topic. This response stated:

> You need to know that the ministry of PK takes no stand on issues like this. In fact, we specifically try to avoid such debates. Our efforts are designed to bring men together based on the historically "essential" doctrines of orthodox Christianity as represented by our Statement of Faith — or to focus on things that unite the body of Christ, instead of those which tend to divide it.
>
> Since different churches and individual Christians hold varying views about creation, it is one of those things we believe falls under the category of "secondary doctrines," just as we do such things as spiritual gifts, eternal security, the rapture, etc. In short, when it comes to subjects like creation, we believe Christians need to extend grace to each other as summed up in the statement: "In essentials, unity. In non-essentials, liberty. In all things, charity."[8]

Now, this is not in any way meant to throw negative asper-sions on the PK movement or its leadership. It is not meant to single them out. It is only that their quote succinctly summarizes a position which is shared by the overwhelming majority of Christian ministries today.

Is creation just one of those "secondary doctrines" like spiritual gifts or the Rapture?

Now, I'm sure that those who make a claim similar to the quote above would agree that the doctrine of creation itself (that God is Creator — Genesis 1:1) is a *primary* doctrine. After all, if God is not Creator, and the first verse of the Bible is not true, then neither is the rest of the Bible. Other than the doctrine of God himself, creation would be *the* most important doctrine, for everything else in Christianity depends on this being true.

When most Christians talk about the doctrine of creation being a secondary doctrine, what they usually mean is the details of the creation account, (i.e., whether the earth is young or old, the days of creation being ordinary days, or Noah's flood being a global event, and so on — these would not be considered es-sential to Christianity).

The details of the creation account *do* matter and are es-sential. If Adam wasn't a real historical figure, then who is our ancestor? How do we know we are sinners? If Adam's fall was *not* a real event in history, then what is sin? If Adam and Eve weren't created just as Genesis records, then the doctrine of marriage is meaningless. If the days of creation aren't ordinary days, then there's no basis for the seven-day week, and God's Word doesn't have to mean what the language clearly states. If the earth is millions of years old, and death, disease, and bloodshed existed before sin, then the gospel is undermined.

The point is that the doctrine of creation is foundational to other doctrines. However, what doctrines are the Rapture or spiritual gifts foundational to?

Creation (i.e., the details in Genesis) is not a "secondary" doctrine — it is in fact foundational to *all* other doctrines.

The world has attacked Christianity and the Word of God by attacking the doctrine of creation — and Christians have basically retreated and compromised with the world's teachings. We need to begin a full-scale training program to equip the troops with the most powerful weapon in the universe — the Word of God.

As part of this training, we also need to understand the thinking of the people we are going to meet. Keeping in mind the basic overall concept of the "Jews" and the "Greeks," what types of people are we going to meet? How can we effectively communicate with them so they will come to a saving faith in the Lord Jesus Christ?

I just want to let you know how much your materials mean to me, as well as your radio outreach. Every Sunday, I gather my wife, two daughters, and son together for a Bible study. I pick out one of the stories in *Creation* magazine and off we go. I use visual aids — a globe and a chalkboard, then I follow through the storyline, pointing out how intricately designed each of the animals, plants, earth, and heavens are. We have a question and answer period afterwards (so I know if the information is sinking in or not), and the last question I always ask is, "And who is the Creator God?" to which my children yell out, "Jesus!"

I need *Creation* magazine and the other Answers In Genesis materials to instill within my children a firm, grounded understanding of the truth of God's Word, shown by the things they can see. I want them to know that the Bible is the truth that they can believe — every word of it — and that evolution is a lie. Thank you for never, ever compromising the truth of God's Word and for fighting the good fight.

O.E., Texas

CHAPTER 11

PRACTICAL CREATION EVANGELISM

W hen I first started teaching in the creation ministry, I would go to churches and speak on scientific aspects such as the age of the earth, the fossil record, and other such topics. People showed some interest, but it certainly didn't seem to stir them with the passion I had for the creation/ evolution topic. And they always seemed to ask the same questions. (You should know them by now!) Where did Cain get his wife? What about the days of creation? How do dinosaurs fit with the Bible?, etc.

One day I read the book *The Genesis Record* by Dr. Henry Morris.[1] It made me realize with a renewed vigor how foundational the Book of Genesis was to the rest of the Bible. As I continued to read, it hit me that I really became excited when I came across an answer to one of the questions I had in my own mind.

It was then that I started to understand that I shouldn't be just giving sermons on what I thought was important. I needed to understand the people to whom I was speaking. Where were they in regard to this topic? What do they think about Genesis? Why don't they think it's that important? Why do they have these questions? What makes them think this way?

I then prepared a sermon to take all this into account. I called it my "Relevance Sermon." It was a 30-minute talk on why Christians should believe in a literal Genesis. I explained how Genesis was foundational to all doctrine and that Christians shouldn't add millions of years to God's Word — that this destroys the foundation of the gospel.[2] I also began to answer questions like the one about Cain's wife. After the service where I preached this for the first time, I was astounded at the response. People seemed to rush out and ask for copies of the tape, and to buy lots of materials. *I had finally communicated!*

As the whole concept of creation evangelism has crystallized in my thinking over the years, I have developed many talks (and materials) to communicate to various groups of people we meet in our everyday life.

The following summarizes some of these groups, giving practical ideas on how to apply creation evangelism.

First of all, I identify a particular group of people. I then try to understand how they think. If their thinking is not firmly founded in God's Word, then they will have major inconsistencies in their way of thinking. I need to identify those inconsistencies, and then carefully dismantle them and show them to be illogical. I then pray the Lord will use this to open their hearts to the truth of God's Word.

Keep in mind that there are many more groups of people than this and some people have characteristics of more than one group. So there are, of course, many exceptions. These are then just generalizations based on my personal experience.

Each of the following diagrams represents a particular group of people.

The first diagram represents where each person should be in relation to his thinking. They start with the Word of God as their foundation, i.e., believing in a literal Genesis as part of this foundation. They have a Christian world view — accepting Christian doctrines, knowing they are *directly* founded on God's Word, and ultimately on Genesis 1–11. Their Christian world view is, in essence, the pair of glasses they use in interpreting everything around them.

Sadly, I have found that most Christians are not in this group. Most people in our churches are in either one of the next two positions — or somewhere in between. If they are in one of these positions, I've found that they really can't defend the Bible against the attacks of the age. The Christian leaders haven't dealt with the "missiles" from the enemy aimed at the Bible, and particularly Genesis.

The next illustration shows that on one side in the church we have: Group 2.

This group represents Christians who believe the Bible is the infallible Word and even generally believe Genesis to be true. They believe in Christian doctrines. However, they don't really understand how their Christian world view connects to the Bible and ultimately to Genesis 1–11. They don't really understand the concept of the Bible being the history book of the universe. This group would also include the classic "gap theorists," who believe God re-created everything in six days, after a gap of millions of years.[3]

For these people, I have summarized the inconsistencies in their thinking as follows:

1. If there is no connection to Genesis, then there is no reason for believing in their doctrines. Because of this lack of

connection, they can't really defend them. They tend to tell their children that marriage is one man for one woman for life — but this is usually forced on them "from the top down" — not built foundationally.

2. These people usually have a wrong understanding of science. They, like most of us, have been indoctrinated to think scientists can prove the earth is billions of years old and that dinosaurs died out millions of years ago. This is one of the reasons why Genesis is not connected to their world view. Even though they generally believe in Genesis, in reality that which they think is science causes them to divorce Genesis from the real world.

3. All these problems result in there being no foundational connection for the next generation. Their children grow up in the Church being taught the Bible is the Word of God. But at the same time, they are not given answers to evolutionary teaching. In fact, they are probably told it's okay to believe in millions of years. The Bible is portrayed to them as separate from their everyday thinking. They may accept doctrines like marriage, but they have no basis for knowing why — except that it's in the New Testament. Ultimately, however, they can't give foundational reasons as to why homosexual behavior, for instance, is wrong.

On the other side in the church we have Group 3:

This group believes the Bible is the Word of God, but they also have no problem adding evolutionary teaching to the Bible. These people may be theistic evolutionists[4] (God used evolution) or progressive creationists[5] (God created millions of species over millions of years) or some other compromise position. They accept major Christian doctrines, but they can be more liberal in the way they apply them. Many, in fact most, Christian college, Bible college, and seminary students — along with their professors — are in this group.

For these people, I have summarized the inconsistencies in their thinking as follows:

1. They not only have no connection for their doctrines, they have no basis for them. The theistic evolutionists, for instance, allow God to use evolution to form man. But this destroys the foundation of marriage which is built on the fact that Eve came from Adam's side. The progressive creationists (like theistic evolutionists) allow millions of years of death, bloodshed, disease, and suffering before sin. Thus, the foundation of the atonement and the restoration is destroyed. Even though they may hold to Christian doctrines, they do so inconsistently, for they don't have a real basis for them.

2. They also have a wrong understanding of science. They equate evolutionary teaching with science. So, there is a need to teach them that the science that put man on the moon can't be used to directly observe the past. Scientists don't have the past to study. Evolution and its teaching of millions of years are really just beliefs.[6]

3. They therefore not only have no foundation for the next generation, they have the *wrong* foundation. At least Group 2 has the right foundation — even if Christians don't understand the connection. However, this group has problems connecting their foundation to doctrine. There are a variety of positions concerning which parts of Genesis are literally true. But ultimately, without a literal Genesis, there is no foundation for any Christian doctrine.

With this group, I have often found that their children will quickly depart from the faith. From my own experience, I've discovered that the children of those in the church who ardently compromise with evolution/millions of years teaching, and are not given answers to defend the inerrancy of Scripture, often have little if anything to do with the Church. There are numerous humanists who claim they once attended Bible-believing churches, but rejected Christianity because of evolution.

For instance, read this testimony of a Harvard professor:

As were many persons from Alabama, I was a born-again Christian. When I was 15, I entered the Southern Baptist Church with great fervor and interest in the fundamentalist religion. I left at 17 when I got to the University of Alabama and heard about evolutionary theory.[7]

Or read this report of an 87-year-old man in North Carolina who was aggressively pursuing legal action to have the Ten Commandments removed from a county courthouse:

He was raised a Methodist in Indianapolis and went to church regularly as a child and teenager. "I believed all this God stuff," he said. "I was a good little boy and all that [expletive]. In school, we opened every morning with the Lord's Prayer. That was big stuff." That changed when he attended Purdue University in Indiana. After taking physics and chemistry, he began to question the veracity of the Bible. In particular, he doubted how the entire world could have flooded in the days of Noah's ark. . . . Where . . . did all that water come from?[8]

Obviously he wasn't given answers to defend the events of Genesis when he went to church. Now, at the end of his life, he was fighting with all his might against the Word of God.

The children in Group 1 tend to stay in the Church — although in a few generations they will begin to lose their Christian heritage if they aren't taught how to defend the Bible in the light of the attacks from secular humanism.

Once we understand where these people are "coming from," we need to construct a program to communicate to them by dealing with these inconsistencies. Whenever I preach in a church for the first time, I assume that I will have people from Group 1 through Group 3, and various stages in between.

We have developed a number of materials to deal with these groups:

1. *The Genesis Solution* film is of myself (with some well-done animation for illustration) preaching a message that deals with each of the inconsistencies listed above.[9] I explain what science is and what it isn't. I also show how all doctrines are founded in a literal Genesis, and the problems when Christians try to add millions of years to the Bible. We explain how important it is to build Christian doctrines from the foundation up. Evolution is shown to be a religion, and the social consequences of evolution are then discussed (also available as a book).

I have found that once I've preached this message in a church, many people will immediately see the importance of Genesis and often change their position to reject millions of years and accept God's Word as written. But this change ultimately depends on their attitude to the Word of God. If they really want to believe God's Word and really want to let God speak to them through the language of the Bible, they are more likely to respond positively. Sadly, academic peer pressure is one of the big stumbling blocks I've found with people holding higher degrees — they are often not prepared to take God at His Word in Genesis. We try to have this film shown in as many churches as possible before we run a seminar in an area, for we find it increases seminar attendance by up to 70 percent. Once Christians realize how important this topic is, they want to know more and have their questions answered.

2. My book *The Lie: Evolution* has the same basic content as the above film, but in more detail.[10] There are many churches that have used this book as a Bible study program for teenagers and adults. The teacher could use *The Genesis Record* as the teacher resource.[11]

3. *The New Answers Book Series* answers the most-asked questions on creation/evolution and the Book of Genesis: Cain's wife, "races," gap theory, dinosaurs, and many more.[12] This can also be used as a Bible study for teenagers and adults.

4. *Creation: Facts of Life* is an important resource book that deals with the major so-called "scientific" evidences for evolution.[13] Dr. Gary Parker, a former evolutionist, used to teach these evidences — now as a creationist, he knows how to

refute them. Thus, this book deals primarily with the science question.

5. For children, our books *A is for Adam*[14] and *D is for Dinosaur*[15] are set up with copious teacher notes in the back to teach all the above concepts not only to children, but teens and adults as well.

6. *Answers in Genesis* video set.[16] This 12-part video series (with a detailed study guide) is a complete video seminar dealing with the biblical and scientific aspects of the origins issue. This is excellent to show to teens and adults.

7. *The Great Dinosaur Mystery Solved!* is an excellent publication that teaches Christians how to think like a Christian (i.e., putting on those biblical glasses) from Scripture.[17] This is then applied practically to dinosaurs, thus teaching young people and adults that they can apply their Christian world view to *every* area.

There are, of course, many other resources that can be used. The Answers in Genesis ministry and other creation ministries are available to help further with recommendations for materials (see addresses at the back of this book).

Group 4 — This group predominantly represents an older generation (what we would probably call "the sixties generation" — the generation which saw prayer taken out of the public schools in America), who were brought up in the culture when it was still rather Christian in philosophy. They usually have a Christian ethic. Mostly they believe marriage should be between a man and a woman. They believe in right and wrong. For many of them, evolution is fact — they see it on TV all the time. They probably wouldn't even question the earth being billions of years old. They tend to be interested in the supernatural, and are worried about the morality of the younger generations. They even believe in God — but they seldom have a personal relationship with Jesus Christ.

For these people, I have summarized the inconsistencies in their thinking as follows:

1. They don't understand that they are holding a Christian ethic in a totally inconsistent way. They may believe in the Christian doctrine of marriage — but why? On what basis would they explain to their son, for example, that living with a woman who seems to be desirable at the time is not right?

In other words, these people have no logical reason to give their children as to why marriage is one man for one woman for life — and why the rightful place for sex is within marriage only. Now this problem exists for *all* Christian-based beliefs they may hold to. This inconsistency can be pointed out time and time again. Why do they believe in right and wrong? Who determines what's wrong? Isn't it just your opinion? Why should their children accept the same morality?

These people also don't realize that the foundation they hold to, evolution, actually is the foundation upon which their children can justify their views on marriage and sex. As we discussed earlier in this book, the foundation of evolution provides the justification for someone to defend abortion, pre-marital sex, and the other social ills.

2. Thus, these people have the *wrong* basis for their world view. If they allow their children to believe in evolution, then it's fully consistent for their children to abandon the morality of their parents.

3. This group also has a wrong understanding of science. Like all the groups, they have been indoctrinated to believe that evolution is science. This needs to be counteracted.

4. The parents among them have laid the *wrong* foundation for the next generation. And those in the next generation usually abandon Christian morality altogether.

Most of those in Group 4 probably attended church or Sunday school at some time in their life. Some of them may even have been regular church attendees, for it was the social thing to do. They may act like Christians, but they aren't truly born again. These people tend to believe that if they go to church and help others, God won't keep them out of heaven.

There's something else I've noticed with members of this group — they tend to ask questions about Cain's wife and the other common questions detailed earlier. Personally, one of the reasons why I believe these people don't ultimately believe the Bible is the infallible, inerrant, Word of God, is because the Church never gave them the answers.

When I was in Phoenix some years ago, I read a letter to the editor in the local newspaper from a man over 70 years old. He said he stopped going to church when he found out he couldn't get an answer as to where Cain got his wife. I found out his phone number and called him and gave him the answer.[18] He was speechless. I prayed he would now reconsider his views about the Bible.

A friend of mine told me about something that occurred next door to him. His 80-year-old neighbor, Bill, was obviously in some trouble. My friend went to him to find out what was wrong. He was having pains in his chest and other symptoms that made it obvious he was having a heart attack. The ambulance was immediately called. My Christian friend had been trying to witness to this man for months. So, he pleaded with Bill to trust the Lord.

Finally, Bill said (and remember, this is while he's having a serious heart attack), "Well if you believe the Bible — where did Cain get his wife?" If it wasn't so serious, this would be very humorous. This again stresses to me the importance of giving answers. Sadly, the Church has not given these basic answers and many have drifted away.

I've found with this group that books like *The New Answers Book* can be of great help in opening doors. Some of our videos (like the Answers in Genesis set or some of the other ones dealing with science) can be very useful in challenging them. This group will

often watch a video if it's left with them. Also, our witnessing books, *Dinosaurs and the Bible, Where Did Cain Get His Wife?* and *Is There Really a God?* can be great to give to them.[19] There are many other resources available to effectively communicate with this group.

Group 5 — This group is made up of university and high school students (or young adults) that are more than likely the sons and daughters of Group 4. For them evolution is fact. They have, by and large, rejected Christian morality. They've grown up in a culture where sexual promiscuity, pornography, and abortion are the norm. Many have emotional problems from abuse during their childhood. They are hurting and don't know how to find healing from this hurt. Many have an intense sense of shame as a consequence of problems in the past. They don't understand what true love is (as Christians understand it). Even those that have gone to church tend to believe in millions of years of suffering before Adam. They can't put it all together. But, at the same time they are crying out for answers. Whenever I give a lecture at a secular university or public school, I have this group in mind.

For these young people, I have summarized the inconsistencies in their thinking as follows:

1. They assume science can prove the past. They, too, like the other groups, have a wrong understanding of the nature of science. This is why the first part of my lecture to this group deals with what real science is and what it isn't. Once they comprehend the

fact that the very science that builds our technology can't be used in the same way to investigate origins, they begin to listen.

2. Their understanding is that evolution is science. They need to grasp that both creation and evolution are *belief* systems. They have been indoctrinated to believe that creation is religion but evolution is science. The late evolutionist Stephen Jay Gould made this a staple argument.

3. They have no understanding that their belief in evolution connects to their entire world view. It is very difficult to try to get them to see the relationship between evolution and abortion, for instance. This is why I don't bring this up until there has been much discussion on points 1 and 2 above. They don't really understand the nature of their thinking. They are like "Greeks" in the sense that they think very differently from their parents (and certainly from Christians). To them, the death and suffering they see around them is part of what life is all about.

4. Usually, among this group, suicide is prevalent. Because of the foundation they have (even though they don't understand how this connects to their world view), they don't see much purpose and meaning in life. This is why they tend to be preoccupied with sex and drugs — these are experiential things to fill the spiritual void in their lives. Even if they went to church at all, they've not been given any real answers.

5. These people are usually shame-driven instead of guilt-driven. They recognize many of their failings — they know they do wrong (their conscience tells them, according to Romans) — and they are emotionally hurt from what has happened to them. Many feel "dirty," but don't know how they can be "clean." They have no solution because they don't understand sin. They will not understand God's love until they understand human origins as given in Genesis.

There are numerous materials available for this group. Sometimes a more technical book might be needed — other times a layman's book. But overall, I always remind people that it's God's Word that will not return unto Him void. I've often found that after dealing with their inconsistencies, by then showing them that I can defend God's Word authoritatively, and presenting the full gospel

(e.g., creation, sin and death, and resurrection) and the change it can make in their life (no more shame), many are interested. They are not used to hearing someone speak with authority in regard to what life is all about.

Group 6 — This group mainly consists of what I call the "academic elite." They would include professors at secular colleges and leaders of humanist groups. They would usually claim to be atheists (or at the very least agnostics — there really are very few practicing atheists). They reject the God of the Bible and are anti-Christian in philosophy. In my opinion, most of them know that evolution is their religion, but they claim it is science. Many know that they have an *a priori* commitment to materialism. Morality is relative to them.

For these people, I have summarized the inconsistencies in their thinking as follows:

1. They have no basis whatsoever for standards of right and wrong. Even though they know this, they can't live like it. They have to accept some things as good and bad, or right and wrong. They can even be very moral people. Thus, one needs to challenge them in regard to the view of ethics they hold on how they can justify this as correct. Eventually, they must come to the conclusion that we do things by consensus if there are no absolutes. However, if they state that there is no such thing as absolute truth, ask them if they are absolutely sure!

2. They assume that evolution is absolute fact. But this could only be so if one knew everything there was to know about everything. In essence, therefore, they are assuming infinite knowledge. They may not have thought this through, but in reality, this is what they are saying. Therefore, they need to be confronted on this. Ask them: "Do you have all evidence to prove conclusively

there is no God?" Ultimately they have to agree they don't. At least this can be a foot in the door with them.

3. They have re-defined science as evolution. When talking with them about science, one would have to ask them to carefully define what they mean. Like all the other groups, they have equated evolution with science. But it can't be the science that provides our technology. They need the same approach as the others: a lecture on the philosophy of science.

4. They have no mechanism for evolution. Materialistic, mechanistic evolution doesn't work. Many scientists have shown that natural selection and mutation (both popularized as the major mechanisms in the evolutionary process) do not add new information into the genes of an organism. Real science has shown there is no mechanism to make evolution work. There are some excellent books written by scientists that deal with this topic in detail.[22]

5. Because there is no materialistic mechanism for evolution, they are lacking something to make it work. Many are now realizing they need a super intelligence to impose information on the system. They don't want the God of the Bible, so they will begin opting for some mystical element as a God substitute. This position is becoming increasingly popular in our culture.

6. Because of this lack of a mechanism, they therefore can't provide a complete foundation for the next generation (their students, or the society as a whole). Thus, the next generation will try to fill this gap.

I have found that the books referenced in point 4 above, ones that deal with information issues, are vital to effectively communicating to this group.

Group 7 — I believe this group represents where our culture is heading. In my opinion, it is probably the hardest group to reach. These people are the products of our universities and public education. They are now starting to get positions of power in the government at local and national levels. As they are the products of the influence of Group 6, they have provided the mystical element they need: the universe (or nature) is "god." This is all part of the New Age religion that is sweeping the world.

Of course, in one sense it's nothing other than a form of Hinduism, but because it's been birthed in our Western culture, it's often entwined with our scientific mindset.

There are, of course, some good Christian books written about the New Age movement. (But be discerning — not all are useful.) There are many things to learn in order to be able to communicate with this group. Nonetheless, evolution is in reality foundational to their thinking. Thus, the same basic arguments used for Groups 5 and 6 should also be applied here. Obviously, if one can get them to see that evolution doesn't work, they should be challenged. Of course, they can always revert to "nature" providing a way, but then they have to defend this logically.

Group 7

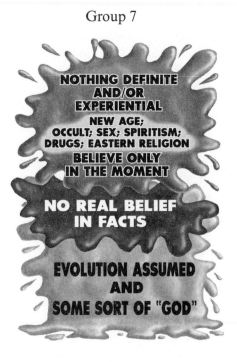

NOTHING DEFINITE AND/OR EXPERIENTIAL
NEW AGE; OCCULT; SEX; SPIRITISM; DRUGS; EASTERN RELIGION
BELIEVE ONLY IN THE MOMENT

NO REAL BELIEF IN FACTS

EVOLUTION ASSUMED AND SOME SORT OF "GOD"

For these people, I have summarized the inconsistencies in their thinking as follows:

1. If "god" is nature, then how can "god" be both good and evil, health and disease, full of joy and suffering? The universe seems very contradictory. It's only the Bible that explains why this is so. The Bible not only explains the origin of evil but also the reason for the existence of death. Because this group of people is interested in supernatural things, sometimes they will listen when you argue authoritatively from the Bible. However, sometimes they will accept what you say and yet accept what they believe at the same time. Because truth is relative, they live in the world inconsistently anyway. They are happy to live illogically and inconsistently.

2. Like some of the Greeks, they believe that a god is part of the creation. Thus, arguments about ultimate causes are important. Again, using information issues, one can give a defense of a Creator outside of (but responsible for) the creation, in contrast to their Creator being a part of the creation.

Some of them, based on their evolutionary beliefs that there is no real distinction between man and animals anyway, are active advocates of animal rights. Many are vegetarian and oppose any animals being killed. Some go so far as to wear masks in case they might kill something (e.g., inhaling microscopic creatures). However, they can't avoid killing creatures in this world, yet another inconsistency in their logic. And who determines whether a bacterium is of more or less value than a dog? Who knows if some mutation in a micro-organism or worm might not lead to a new evolutionary sequence? Actually, if all evolutionists were consistent, they should have such a movement as a "Save the tapeworm society." Just because an organism causes a disease which is inconvenient for us, does that mean we should kill it? Maybe in the grand scheme of things from an evolutionary perspective, we should leave it alone! Perhaps humans should be prepared to die out and let something else evolve to an even higher state?

One should always try to push evolutionists to the logical conclusions of their presuppositions.

3. Like many of the Eastern religions, tradition overrules reason. No matter how you reason with them, the religion they've chosen usually overrules what they hear. However, as discussed earlier in the book, we must do our best to reason with them, and then leave it to the Holy Spirit to convict and convert.

When witnessing to such people, as well as giving answers, we need to be like Christ and ask pertinent questions. We should always be thinking in terms of the inconsistencies in their logic. Then we should ask a question that deals with this. If one can get a person to see how inconsistent they are, this can be a tremendous challenge for them to re-think their position.

At one seminar, a young man came up to me and said, "I'm an atheist. As an atheist I don't believe in any absolutes. In fact,

PRACTICAL CREATION EVANGELISM

we can't even be sure of reality. To be honest I can't even prove I'm here."

"In that case, why are you even asking me any questions?" I replied.

"Good point," said this young man.

"What point?" I stated.

"Maybe I should go home," he said.

"Maybe it's not there," I retorted.

"Good point," he replied.

"What point?" I exclaimed.

He smiled and said, "I'll think about it."

At another seminar, a young man came up to me and said, "Well, I sat through your talks, but I still believe in evolution and the big bang. I don't believe in God. I still think we got here by chance."

I replied to him, "Well, if you evolved by chance, then your brain evolved by chance — if your brain evolved by chance, then your processes of logic evolved by chance. If that's true, you can't be sure your logic evolved the right way. Son, you don't even know if you're asking me the right questions."

And his reply? "Can you tell me the name of the book you just recommended?"

In an anthropology class, my teacher wrote on the board: *Creation (based on faith, stories) — Evolution (fact)*. Then he said, "Evolution is considered fact, but the theory is still being worked out." At one point, he said, "I think humans are a freak mutation. Our brains grew, and who knows how it happened."

On the first day of class, this same teacher told my friend's class, "If you believe [in] God, you might as well forget it — He doesn't exist." These are just several experiences I have had in the past. My family subscribes to the *Technical Journal* and *Creation* magazine. I just wanted to write and let you know the great influence you have had in my life. It has helped me to understand creation and the validity of the Bible. I have been able to help others with this topic and give them another view besides society's view.

During the summer, I work for youth group camps and am in contact with many youths with questions. I am happy to let you know that what I have learned is being passed on to others to enlighten them to the truth. Keep up the wonderful work because it is well worth it and it has touched many lives. Thank you sincerely.

J.K., Michigan

Today I rejoiced with the angels in heaven when my son David prayed that his name would be in the Lamb's Book of Life. We had read *A Is for Adam* through for the third time when he asked if his name was written in there. Then he wanted to pray. We made a note in the front of his Bible as a reminder.

We love the books and videos from AiG. Thank you and God bless you.

K.H., Australia

CHAPTER 12

THE GENERATION GAPS

As a final challenge to the Church, I want to once more go over the seven major groups, but in a slightly different way. I am going to use America (because it did start as a Christian nation) to illustrate this important point.

Group 1 — Most of the founding fathers in America would have been more like this. Perhaps generations ago, most Christians in America would have been (or should have been) like this group.

Group 1

But over time, people began to be influenced by evolutionary teaching and indoctrinated to believe in millions of years. More and more people became like Groups 2 and 3.

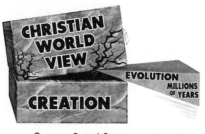

Groups 2 and 3

Now the foundation of the Christian faith was being compromised, and cracks started to appear in the Christian framework. The connection of their thinking to the Bible started to be removed.

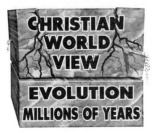

Group 4

The next few generations became more consistent with their compromised foundation, or lack of connection to a foundation, and many became a part of Group 4.

This group has lost all connection to the Bible, but still tries to maintain a Christian way of thinking to a degree. But their children build a way of thinking that's consistent with the foundation their parents gave them. Thus we arrive at Group 5.

This group provides the professors and leaders for the next generations, and they depart totally from a Christian way of thinking. Group 6 then takes over our universities and colleges.

Group 5

Group 6

The next generation sees the inconsistency of not having a driving "force" (an intelligence to make it work) to account for the universe and life, and so they turn to the New Age movement (Group 7).

This group is very difficult to reach with the gospel message. Their situation is the ultimate end of totally losing the foundation of the Word of God.

Now I want to give you two examples to illustrate this same sequence applied to families:

Group 7

1. In a sense, some people could say: Great Grandpa — he was in Group 1. Yes, but his children were in Groups 2 and 3. And their children were in Group 4. And the next generation is in Group 5 or 6. Look at the great grandson (Group 7) — he's humming, with crystals, on mountains — a real New Ager. This is basically what has been happening to the culture in America and other Western nations.

> IF THE BIBLE CLEARLY STATES GOD CREATED IN SIX DAYS — WHICH IT DOES — THEN WHEN A THEOLOGIAN RECOGNIZES THIS, BUT RE-INTERPRETS THE DAYS TO FIT WITH MILLIONS OF YEARS, THIS HAS UNLOCKED A DOOR.

2. How many Christian schools have maintained the faith of their founders? Very, very few. In fact, they've gone through the same basic sequence. I believe that colleges started by Christians or churches can also be classified into one of those 7 groups. There are many that are well on the way to becoming Group 7 — many have already reached Group 6.

And how did that change occur? There are many complicated reasons of course. But overall, there's no doubt that the absolute authority of God's Word was eroded by evolutionary teaching (that man determines truth independent of revelation), as more and more people compromised with God's Word.

As I've stated before: If the Bible clearly states God created in six days — which it does — then when a theologian recognizes this, but re-interprets the days to fit with millions of years, this has unlocked a door. The theologian has just told his students that God's Word is *fallible*. The erosion has begun!

Any Christian college that compromises its foundation in the Bible beginning with Genesis (and this sadly is the state for most) has started on that slippery slide of unbelief that leads to the destruction of any Christian thinking at all. This to me is the *real* generation gap!

This all seems so depressing. Can the tide be turned? Only if God's people understand these foundational changes and use

God's methods to make the change back. But the mountain of evolution and compromise is so great. Isn't it too late?

I once said to someone, "If you start digging a coal mine with a teaspoon, you will gradually make a small hole. But, if you get millions of people with teaspoons, the hole will grow to an enormous one." The modern creation movement is about 30 years old. Thankfully, there are many across the world who are digging away at the foundations of evolution and compromise. And it is making a big difference.

Most of us are familiar with the story of David and Goliath. In that battle, which took place nearly 3,000 years ago, we are told that the brutish giant, Goliath, when he saw David coming toward him, "Disdained him; for he was but a youth, and ruddy, and of fair countenance" (1 Sam. 17:42). David's response? "Thou comest to me with a sword, and with a spear, and with a shield, but I come to thee in the name of the Lord of hosts, the God of the armies of Israel, whom thou hast defied" (1 Sam. 17:45). The result? The giant was slain!

How easy it is to become depressed and dejected when one sees the "giants" that array themselves against any ministry like Answers in Genesis, or any individual who takes a stand for a literal Genesis. But take heart, for like Goliath, they can be defeated, with God's help. Let us consider two classes of "giants" and view them from a biblical perspective.

1. "Non-Christian giants" — These may include the news media, secular universities and colleges, humanist organizations, governments, etc. It is easy to feel defeated and discouraged when one sees the massive propaganda machines that have been set up to indoctrinate billions of people with evolutionary philosophy. What can be done to fight people who are highly qualified and are world-renowned experts? Many of us identify with David. We feel like children compared to some of these intellectual "giants." What can we do to combat what they are doing?

2. "Christian giants" — The creation message not only gets opposition from non-Christians, but also from Christians. Many lecturers in well-known theological colleges have written articles or books against the straightforward, creationist position that

many Christians hold. It is easy for the average Christian to feel intimidated by Christian scholars of such great qualification and position. In fact, there are many Christians who listen to such people and accept what they are saying because they are impressed by their "scholarship."

Many such academics in our Christian colleges and churches seem to be motivated by a desire for acceptance and respect from their secular peers. It is a great temptation to want respect from non-Christian intellectuals. Unfortunately, we often forget that when sin defaced the image of God back in the Garden of Eden, it marred man's ability to think, also. What we all need to be asking ourselves is whether it is this mentality from which we want respect, or do we seek to please God?

In 2 Corinthians 11:3, Paul warns us not to "be corrupted from the simplicity that is in Christ." It is often claimed that to accept Genesis literally, i.e., a straightforward reading, is too simplistic. Instead, we are often told to listen to the academics and theologians of the day in their explanation of what it really means. A good example of this is seen in the writings of Dr. Pattle P.T. Pun, from the Department of Biology at Wheaton College in Illinois. He stated, "It is apparent that the most straightforward understanding of the Genesis record, *without regard to all of the hermeneutical considerations suggested by science*, is that God created heaven and earth in six solar days, that man was created in the sixth day, that death and chaos entered the world after the fall of Adam and Eve, that all of the fossils were the result of the catastrophic universal deluge which spared only Noah's family and the animals therewith"[1] (emphasis ours).

What Pun is saying, of course, is that a straightforward reading of Genesis suggests it means exactly what it says! It teaches a literal six-day creation, Fall, and Flood. However, noting the sentence we emphasized in his quote tells you that he is insisting we must accept what secular scientists of our day are saying about the subjects and must re-interpret the Bible to fit their theories.

However, God has called those of us who are His children to seek out *His* praise — not the praises of men! Praise God that there still are many highly qualified people who accept the Genesis account, who have the heart of David, and who understand that the fear of God is the beginning of wisdom and knowledge. Let God's enemies rant and rave, but let us give glory to God. Let us not be afraid of "giants." After all, the evidence, rightly interpreted, is on our side, no matter what some of the academics and theologians of the day may say. What we need to do is to communicate this easy-to-understand evidence to a population that has been indoctrinated by self-styled "giants." Like David, with God on our side and faith in His Word, we can defeat these "giants."

Creation evangelism — this is one of the most powerful and necessary tools for God's people today. The next chapter will encourage you and give hope and show that the "giant" can be defeated!

We appreciate your ministry. Creation science is what brought my husband to Christ. As home-schooling parents, we're thankful for the opportunity to protect our children from evolutionary brainwashing. They love *Creation* magazine. We donated our "used" copies to the church library so that others can benefit from the sound, attractively presented teaching.

J.G., Oregon

CHAPTER 13

"MYTH-ING" THE POINT

Have you ever noticed that when the topic of evolution, or millions of years, comes up, there's an incredible emotional reaction? Why? Because that's where the enemy has gained ground; this is where the battle is at.

After all these years, I'm still amazed that the Christian community largely misses the direction of the battle for the hearts and minds of men, women, and children.

As I've stated, ministries like Answers in Genesis are frequently accused of being divisive. I must press the point, however, that the foundational parts of the Bible are the real key.

If we don't agree that the Bible teaches six literal days, if we allow ourselves to be influenced by the millions of years, and we don't read the text as written . . . right there in Genesis 1, we've lost the battle. The battle is lost because the message to the people is, "We don't have to take the Bible seriously here." That compromise opens a door that leads to disaster.

In his autobiography, retired Episcopal bishop John Shelby Spong provides us with a bird's-eye view of his spiritual "evolution." Tragically, this man's loss of faith has imperiled countless others, for the simple reason that Spong is so popular with the media. Evangelical pastors might preach a message of the Cross, but the young people in their congregations will likely see Spong on their college campus or on television programs like "Politically Incorrect." There he will tear into the whole Bible. Spong is famous for his bold dissections of Scripture, and this has led him to his defense of abortion, homosexual practices, and re-interpretation of Christianity. The bishop does not believe in the Virgin Birth or the Resurrection, and he has endorsed the radical scholars' contention that many of the New Testament quotes attributed to Christ were in fact made up by the apostles.

But this is the point where Spong's experience gets really interesting. Guess where his doubts about the Bible and Christianity first surfaced? As a seminary student.

Spong describes his experiences in zoology classes, where he was mentored by Dr. Claiborne Jones. The professor was, according to Spong, "the first Darwinian Christian I had ever met."[1] In the beginning, the young Spong made a stand for the Bible.

"In those classes I tried to defend the literal creation story against Darwin's theory. Claiborne Jones was always gracious, but even I knew that I had lost that fight."[2]

The rest of the book is a frightening account of a man who abandoned orthodox Christianity, and who now uses his position of influence to encourage others to do the same.

The history in Genesis 1–11 is foundational to the rest of the Bible. If you wanted to get rid of Christianity, what's the best way to do it? The best way would be to get rid of the history, because once the history is gone, it's then just some pie-in-the-sky religion, divorced from its foundation. Ultimately it will collapse.

That's exactly what's happened.

It's fairly obvious that our culture today is post-Christian. Rape, embezzlement, infidelity, the most heinous murders — these and many more wrongs are increasingly rampant, compared to just a few generations ago. The real reason is because our foundation has been undermined.

Christians are out in the culture saying that abortion is wrong, homosexual behavior is wrong, and do you know what the world is saying? They're saying, "What are you talking about? Science has proved that the Bible can't be trusted, so its outdated 'rules' aren't for me."

But here we are in the Church preaching Christian morality. The world understands this connection, or, rather, disconnection. If the Bible isn't true in some parts, Christianity offers no hope to anyone.

Popular talk show host Larry King made an interesting statement in *World* magazine. He talked about problems he had with the Bible (and, evidently, no one ever helped him with these difficulties): "The God of the Old Testament, I didn't like the things He did . . . I remember thinking, *Why would He [ask Abraham to sacrifice his son]? As a test?* So I said to myself, *I don't know. I just don't know.* That's still true to this day."[3]

Larry King deserves answers! The truth is, almost the whole culture resembles Larry King. There are millions of people walking around, looking for peace and an answer to their problems.

The Church today is recognizing there's a problem; we're not connecting with the world. Yet most leaders and even lay people are loath to look at the foundational issues.

Kenneth Carder, the resident bishop of Mississippi for the United Methodist Church, was relating a perplexing problem to the denomination's board of discipleship. Carder lamented the decline of a "once-prominent" church in Mississippi whose membership had dwindled over the course of a century from 1,000 to 17. Now the church was closing. According to an article from the United Methodist News Service: "Noting that the church used official United Methodist resources, rituals, and curriculum, had won an award for evangelism and was Methodist to the core, the bishop wondered why it was closing and what it had missed. The answer, he said, was that the church was in a neighborhood in transition and had not reached out to the people around it."[4]

No, that church closed precisely because of the reasons cited earlier: it used UMC resources and curriculum, and it "was Methodist to the core."

Don't misunderstand me; I'm not picking on the United Methodist Church. An important point needs to be made, though. If you're an individual, a church, or a denomination, and you say that we don't have to agree on the literal six days of creation, you've lost the battle. You've lost your churches, literally.

Think about it. If the events of Jesus Christ's birth, death, and resurrection didn't happen in history, then how can we be saved? If we all don't go back to one man in history, a literal man in a literal garden (and many mainline churches do not believe this), then who are we? Where did we come from?

As I travel and speak, I do sometimes get depressed when I talk to Christian leaders who tell me that Genesis is a metaphor. If Genesis is a metaphor, what about the account of Adam and Eve? Well, it's a metaphor. If it's a metaphor, then what about the genealogies in the Bible? In the New Testament and in Chronicles, you'll notice something. All of these genealogies — of real people — are traced directly to Christ. So you're telling me that this real person goes back to that real person, who goes back to another real person who goes back to . . . a metaphor?

This is the tortured, convoluted message given by our modern churches to a hurting world searching for answers. It's perhaps a wonder that many congregations last as long as they do.

Do you have any idea what kind of scholarship has been influencing our churches for over a hundred years?

In the 18th and 19th centuries, some in the new field of geology began to assign long ages to the earth, realizing this would undermine the biblical record. Sadly, it was the clergy that rushed to embrace this new philosophy, and we see today the sorry outcome.

The Interpreter's Bible, a commentary set that came into the mainline churches like a tidal wave, was dominated by writers who assigned Genesis to the realm of myth. Men like Walter Russell Bowie (who would influence a young Jack Spong) introduced the subtly blasphemous idea that the Bible was influenced by Babylonian myth. This teaching opened up an assault on the Christian faith that has only intensified.

This literature in turn has worked its leaven into modern curricula. So should we be surprised when churches like the one in Mississippi close their doors? What is the point of going to church, when church leaders basically state that the history upon which the entire life-transforming message of Christianity is based is really a bunch of campfire stories?

All through books like *The Interpreter's Bible*, we are sooth-ingly assured that Genesis 1–11 does not have to be taken literally. In all this, somehow, leaders are baffled over the sharp declines in church membership and even attendance.

When the historical connection to the "genesis" of sin is severed, the results are predictable.

A 1998 Associated Press reporter perhaps unwittingly il-lustrated this fact. An article appeared, detailing Sunday services at Foundry United Methodist Church in Washington, D.C., the home church of President and Mrs. Bill Clinton.[5]

Embroiled in the scandal of his affair with a White House intern, Bill Clinton joined other parishioners in listening to the sermon of Rev. Philip Wogaman. The reverend, a champion of liberal causes on many fronts, was defending the president. Oddly, Wogaman alluded to Genesis: "A number of things have been hap-pening this week. Some would say: 'Is this the time for an academic sermon on the Bible?' Isn't it exactly right for us to be looking at the Bible? The Bible is about human beings and their humanity and it is directed at human beings in their humanity."

According to the article, "Wogaman drew a distinction be-tween taking the Bible seriously and taking it literally. Referring to the story of Adam and Eve and the Garden of Eden, Woga-man said the truths the story illuminates are what's important, not the literal facts given in the story." Or, as Wogaman put it, "There is a difference between fact and truth."

With logic like this from prominent religious leaders, it shouldn't surprise us that moral relativism has enveloped the culture.

Mainline church leaders are not the only ones who distort Genesis, thus losing their position of moral influence. In a series of interviews in the mid-1990s, television producer Hugh Hewitt interviewed several of the leading religious leaders of our day. One particularly fascinating interview was with Charles Colson, the founder of Prison Fellowship.[6]

Midway through the interview, Hewitt asked, "The creation story — seven days — do you believe that?" Colson then launched into a strange answer:

The Bible is not like any other book, but you have to read it like any other book. Parables are parables. Poetry is poetry. Metaphors are metaphors. Allegories are allegories. Where you have to be careful (and scholars spend a lot of time on this) is reading a didactic teaching as didactic teaching, reading historical accounts as clearly historical accounts, and reading parables as parables. When it says that the heavens declare the glory of God, well, we know that the heavens don't speak. We use the same kinds of expressions in modern American language. We say the mountains clap their hands. We say that the sun rises. But the sun doesn't rise. Obviously. We know that. But that's a figure of speech. And the Bible is replete with figures of speech that people could understand. And they have to be read as figures of speech. Now, you asked specifically about the seven days. No, I believe that those are seven ages. Actually, I don't think it matters whether it was seven literal days or not.

You see, Colson has, despite good intentions, unlocked a door. He's allowing thinking and beliefs about long ages, based on presuppositions from outside the Bible — ones which are anti-God to the core — to influence his understanding of history, which in turn influences the way he approaches the Bible in this area. A follow-up question from Hewitt, regarding why God would allow suffering, elicited a sad, but understandable, answer from Colson: "I don't know."

How can he give an answer, because if you believe in long ages, you MUST believe that death and suffering could NOT have only entered the world after Adam's sin, as we have shown.

You see, we've disconnected the Bible from reality. The world sees this, but the Church doesn't.

There is much work to be done.

As always, my thoughts go back to the only source of truth we have.

In the great Book of Isaiah, chapter 66, verse two, we read of a sobering reality: "But to this man will I look, even to him that is poor and of contrite spirit, and trembleth at my word."

God himself is telling us that the person who gives proper respect to Scripture will find that he is pleasing the Lord. If we truly fear God, the Creator, then we realize that we don't have the right to change His Word. Sadly, this practice is very common in the Church.

Adding man's fallible ideas to the Bible has left the Church almost impotent in many places. The first false step was "re-imagining" Genesis; after that, the world saw our hypocrisy and left our pews and Bible study groups to find meaning in other religions and other quests.

Perhaps you are a pastor. I know how difficult that special calling can be. It's tough at times. Whether you are struggling with a tiny congregation or a mega-church in turmoil, I urge you to come back to the whole Word of God. In your office, prayerfully consider using creation evangelism. I'm not saying all your problems will disappear, but if we are a people of the Book — if we say that the Bible is our rock, our touchstone of truth, turn to it unashamedly. Make it the foundation of your thinking in every area, and begin to lead your congregation along that path.

Whoever we may be, we need to ask ourselves, "Where is our allegiance? To the Words of God, or the plans, programs, and opinions of mere men? Whom do *we* tremble at?"

CHAPTER 14

THE VICTORY CHAPTER!

S alvation testimonies, changed lives, and personal impact
stories. The results of creation evangelism:

Dear Answers in Genesis:

Thank you for your faithfulness to God and to the defense of
His Word and the gospel of Jesus Christ. I was a religious Baptist
and an evolutionist (B.S. in geology), and had a false conversion
as a child. Thanks to the modern creationist movement, I now
am certain of my salvation by faith in Jesus Christ alone.
Thank you for answering God's call to return the church's
confidence in all of the Bible.
E.C., Clayton, NC

I started a creation organization at my university in Iowa this
year. We showed the video *Evolution: Fact or Belief.* We drew a
moderate crowd with about six ardent evolutionists going "pssst"
every time something was mentioned that they didn't like. Later
on, two evolutionary atheists became believers in Jesus Christ!
I am very much in favor of your message and style and would
like to be considered a satellite group to your organization.
T.B., Iowa

I was saved as a result of being convinced that evolution was a lie and, hence, was led to read Genesis and the rest of the Bible.

R.L., California

Thank you for all the great things you do! I am a biology major and am constantly bombarded with evolutionary theory. I must admit that my faith was very much damaged until I came across your ministry on the radio. Your ministry exposed me to highly educated Christian scientists who also believe in the Bible. This type of exposure helped restore my faith.

I particularly enjoyed the cassette where Ken and a physicist from New Mexico defended creationism. . . . Thanks, again, for confronting evolution head on and in doing so, giving honor to our Lord and Savior, Jesus Christ.

J.S., Michigan

Thank you for the donation of these books in Russian. We have reached out to the Russian Jews of Indianapolis for four years now. Few have been saved (until now). Yesterday, two Russian Jews accepted the Messiah! Thanks, again.

L.C., Indiana

I am currently a student at the University of Cape Town and am very interested in acquiring the video series *Answers in Genesis* featuring Ken Ham and Dr. Gary Parker. The work that you have been doing was very instrumental in my coming to know the Lord Jesus in 1994.

J.L., South Africa

Hi. I'm from Leonard. I thank you for sending me your newsletter. It has really changed my life. I used to not care about Christians or God or anything religious. But since I've been getting the newsletters, I have started going to church, listening to Christian music. I gave the Lord my life and I have joined our youth witness program. I want to thank you for helping me achieve all of these goals. Would you pray for me?

Thank you so much. I will continue to pray for you and AiG.

H.E., Texas

You may possibly remember me, as I gave you a **BBC** *Wildlife* magazine, in which I had written for creation against [evolutionary] theory at Liverpool two years ago. You gave me a *Creation Technical Journal* and remarked that I had the better of the bargain. Quite correct, and I am pleased to be able to tell you that was the start of me getting saved and becoming a young earth/6-literal-day creationist. Praise the Lord!

P.S., United Kingdom

I'm putting together a presentation for our youth group at church based on Ken Ham's lectures and books. I'm hoping to reach a young man who has been wooed away from his faith by a biology teacher who has convinced him that evolution is fact and the Bible is just stories. Thanks for your ministry.

You were instrumental in my fiancé (a former evolutionist and atheist) to accept Jesus. When he heard Ken Ham's lectures here in Boise last month, that was the last question answered and he accepted Jesus. We are now in pre-marital counseling with my pastor.

T.C., Iowa

We love your material and your home page [www.Answers-InGenesis.org] on the Internet. I have found several articles here that we have been able to use to help point people to Christ.

B.N., associate pastor

Thank you for praying for my brother Steve. Your handwritten note was such a surprise and comfort to me.

Praise Report! My brother and I had a long overdue talk. After several hours of listening and witnessing, I said, "Come on, let's pray." This 240-pound ex-marine drill instructor wept like a baby in my arms asking Jesus to forgive him.

Praise God. Thank you for your love and support. I love you all!
D.M., Georgia

Your ministry revitalized my faith and has been wonderful for equipping me to defend my faith. Your ministry brought my brother to Christ and now he is raising godly children.
J.H., Arkansas

Thank you for all the resources you make available to the general public. Through you, God has really changed my way of thinking.

Two years ago, I graduated from Ohio State University with a bachelors' degree in geologic sciences. Unfortunately, as with most colleges, I learned only uniformitarianism/evolutionary geology. Though I didn't agree with ape-to-man theory, I agreed with all of the other ideas. However, thanks to God, I began to question both creationism —about which I knew nothing — and evolution. I have AiG to thank for providing me books on rocks, fossils, and other scientific differences in creationism and evolution. I now teach kids of all ages the truth.
C.R., Kentucky

Our church bought the *Answers in Genesis* video series when you were in Denver some years back. Recently in pre-marital counseling, these tapes were an effective tool in the salvation of the prospective husband.
D.G., pastor, Colorado

I have enjoyed your videos and books for some time now. Your organization was immensely important in leading me to faith.
R.G., Tennessee

Your magazine has played a big part in a workmate of mine becoming a Christian. It is still helping him with encouragement and has answered many of this man's questions. Thank you and God bless you.
J.K., Australia

I would like to let you know how much your teaching has transformed me. You really set the right foundation for me. You so clearly explain creation that the ones who hear are "without excuses." I've been feeding myself with *Creation* magazine and the *Answers in Genesis* video series. Both are excellent works that glorify our Creator and Lord Jesus Christ. I must have watched the videos at least ten times.

I followed your advice and started teaching our four children (ages 2 to 6) from Genesis 1:1. It totally changed them. My son recently said, "Thank you, Jesus, that you made me." My wife and I had tears of joy realizing that the last six months of teaching had paid off.

R.B., Canada

After an Answers in Genesis seminar, one lady wrote, "Thank you, God, for bringing me back into life." One young man, Darren, who had never heard the creation message before, listened throughout the whole day. He is not a Christian, but said that the seminar was excellent. He has been reading *The Lie: Evolution* and another creation book throughout the week and he has also taken creation videos from our library. He is showing incredible interest and came to church on Sunday — he has really been challenged to become a believer.

We are praying and believing for him to soon be the Lord's, if he's not already. Also a Japanese lady read *The Lie: Evolution* in Japanese. She went to the seminar on Sunday and told me the next day she understands it clearly and now believes the creation message.

R.H., pastor in Australian church

One evening I was reading *A Is for Adam,* to [my grandchildren] at bedtime, for perhaps the 15th time since buying the book at a convention in 1996. This time, however, five-year-old Ana stopped me when we reached "P is for Plan." First, she recounted the entire plan as found there and then asked, "When we're all finished reading the book, will you please pray with me so that I may be really sure that my name is written in the Lamb's Book of Life?"

After reviewing the Plan, once again, to be sure she really understood, we prayed together for Ana to receive Christ as her Savior. Later, I printed her name in the Book of Life opposite the letter "L" to serve as a reminder that on July 30, 1997, Ana entered the fellowship of believers.

C.S., Michigan

I want to thank you for your ministry and your clear common sense presentations relating to Genesis and your bold defense of the accuracy of the whole Bible. My faith has been tremendously strengthened. Those old familiar verses now daily take on deeper meanings, as I ponder them afresh through the lenses of "biblical creationism" which are being continually polished. Everything continues to make more and more sense as I replace the flawed material in my "foundation" with the Master's handiwork.

What a breath of fresh air, what amazing revelation has come as a result.

E.G., North Carolina

We may never know how God has used our efforts to help people come to a belief in the truth given in His Word.

S.R., Colorado

Thanks for all that you are doing. The information and resources I gather from AiG are absolutely central to my efforts to do a good job raising my eight-year-old son and central to just surviving and keeping my focus on God's Word in this crazy secular world.

It is such a blessing to financially support the ministry of AiG. I can never give enough to show the gratitude I feel to the Lord for giving us the AiG ministry in this time of global famine for His Word!!

We're having a great time going through all the new resources, too—especially the extraordinary *Great Dinosaur Mystery Solved* book, and the chock-full of incredible information tract *Is there Really a God?* Wow! And we just discovered the *The X-Nilo Show* —working on getting public access play for it here. My son wears his *Evolution: The Lie* and *Missionary Lizards* shirts everywhere — a real salt-n-light kid in this Charlottesville area.

It was such a great blessing to spend an extended time with the Hams and Parkers and to realize how sacrificial their efforts are. They never mentioned it, of course, and we don't really get a sense of it in the regional seminars, but to see them in their family context and to get a glimpse of the scope of the ministry and the unbelievable amount of time that has been invested in reversing a century-old, culturally imbedded, totally false belief system — these beautiful servants — well, I'm at a loss for words. Surely the effort is very much a Noah's ark. It must seem at times that the task was insurmountable, yet look at the effects your persistent voice has given to reversing the damage of evolutionary indoctrination.

AiG and its international counterparts are truly the John the Baptists for pre-revival reformation, preparing the Darwin-contaminated soil to receive the seed of the gospel.

E.W., Virginia

I wanted to write and thank you for your dedication to a difficult and often despised ministry.

Twenty-five years ago I attended a Christian college which, like most Christian colleges, taught theistic evolution. This teaching came mostly through a philosophy professor who ridiculed the idea that the "Bible could dictate to science." This, along with some chinks in the Bible department, left me extremely confused. This confusion paralyzed my Christian life for years, had me dabbling with New Age ideas in the eighties, and is still a source of guilt and regret for me. I recently felt it necessary to write to the college when I heard they were hosting a public "debate" on evolution. The college president wasn't rude, but refused to acknowledge my problem, taking the usual line that the issue is not an important one . . . that the college must keep an open mind. That the college must be nice and not dogmatic . . . all of those things you have undoubtedly heard a thousand times. I found it to be an emotionally draining experience.

While it was only an academic matter to them, for me it meant facing the loss of many years of my life during which I was "taken captive by hollow and deceptive philosophy."

I now regularly support AiG (and not my alma mater). I recently got a copy of your tape *Challenge to the Church,* and found it most illuminating and uplifting, but it was discouraging to know how big the problem of evolution in the Church really is. Your comment about "seeing so many kids destroyed by their Christian colleges" really jumped out at me. Now, I want to find others who have endured similar experiences and form a support group — perhaps called "Middle-aged people whose youthful faith was torpedoed at their Christian college" or something like that.

I have been on the right track in my Christian life for ten years now, but I still struggle with the past. I struggle with discerning how to teach my children in order to help them avoid some traps. I started late with them, but am trying to make up for lost time. Please pray for us. God bless you abundantly.

D.D., Nevada

Even though I know and have known for many years that the Bible is true, your seminar made me look at things differently somehow. It gave me a new excitement and Bible study seems more adventurous — not only Genesis, but all of the Word of God. I thank you for that.

K.J., New Mexico

The Answers in Genesis seminar and ministry is incredible! God bless you for making it so much fun to go back to Genesis and defend the Word of God. I pray you will come back to Denver again.

T.S., Colorado

I am a music teacher of piano and guitar. A while back a young man named Mike became a student of mine. He was a Christian and loved Jesus. During our lessons, we had many discussions about faith. His high school biology class was daily indoctrinating him with evolution. I gave him materials from AiG and he bought additional things from your ministry.

That boy pored over those materials, sometimes only getting two hours of sleep a night. He asked his biology teacher to let him present the creation viewpoint in class. Although the teacher hesitated, he eventually let him do it. That boy was prepared, and when he stood before the class, God gave him perfect calmness. He was able to present the creation viewpoint without any embarrassment, stumbling, or awkwardness. He believes God empowered him. Many students asked him a lot of questions, and the teacher asked to borrow the materials and read them.

Just thought you'd like to know. Your work is not in vain.

L.K., Ohio

This is an excellent [web] site [www.AnswersInGenesis.org]! God bless you all so much. I never could find science facts like this on site before. If only I could have had this in high school, it would have saved me years in my search for truth. God bless you all so much.

Ken (no last name)

Last week I received in the mail an audio tape of Ken Ham entitled *Challenge to the Church — Calling Christians Back to the Authority of the Bible.* I drive a truck for a living and listened to it on my vehicle's stereo. As I listened again and again, I said, "Wow! This is just what we need to hear!"

On Wednesday, I called AiG and asked them to rush ten copies to my house for my class on Sunday. I put together a special class using materials from AiG. It was a big hit.

You've got some big fans at my church now.

Please pray that the Lord will move hearts to permit us to hold more classes so we can reach a wider portion of the congregation.

D.R., Maryland

Thank you for teaching us to compare, analyze, question, and compare all information against the plain truth stated plainly in God's perfect Word! My children were even able to pick up on erroneous teaching during an astronomy presentation.

S. R., Colorado

My husband, three children, and I attended your seminar in Saginaw and our lives have been greatly affected by the creation message. . . . I've always been a scientifically minded person, yet I've always believed in the truth of God's Word. For years, I struggled to reconcile the evolutionary teaching I had received with the Bible. I don't struggle anymore! I really appreciate your unwillingness to compromise or water down your message. I also appreciate your firm stand against evolutionary thinking in the church, even when it shows up in some of the most respected leaders. We pray for you daily.

M.E., Michigan

This is the first letter I've ever written to any ministry, but I do so with a grateful heart.

I've been a Christian for almost five years. I had the opportunity to attend one of your seminars in Lansing. What a blessing it was and continues to be. Not only did it rekindle my interest in the creation/evolution issue, but it ignited a passion in me to search and study the Scriptures more deeply. Your printed materials and tapes have been one of God's greatest tools for strengthening my walk of faith. Not only have I learned from such rich resources, but I've had many chances to share the importance of belief in a literal and historical Genesis. I often find myself devouring many of the books I order and referring back to them often.

Know that you are all in my prayers often, since I see all around me so much of the evolutionist/humanist world view — even sadly enough, in so many of God's churches. Your resources continue to remind me that what Christ's church needs more than slick programs and contemporary music is a return to the authority of God's Holy Word.

M.M., Michigan

I am a 5th year student at Eastern Illinois University studying psychology with a minor in history. I attended a seminar in Danville, Illinois, a month ago, and am so grateful I did. My eyes were opened and God showed me light, but along with that light, I have seen much evil being taught at my school, even by "believers."

M.M., Illinois

I'm a pastor and appreciate the influence your ministry has had on a number of the members of our church, especially the home schoolers. Thank you.

D.W., New York

In our 10th grade honors biology class at a public high school, we are researching the case for creation. Our biology textbooks claim that evolution is the basis for all life. We are in need of information that can be used to show our classmates the improbability of evolution, and scientific evidence for creation. Any materials that you could provide such as pamphlets, posters, etc., would be greatly appreciated. We hope that you can help us expand our knowledge.

T.C., L.F., and G.B.
(teenagers at a public high school)

I am a college student on a secular campus. AiG has been an answer to prayer, a faith builder, and a real blessing. Thank you very much.

Ray (no last name)

First of all, I just want to thank you for your ministry. My faith has been strengthened greatly during my high school years through your ministry.

A friend of mine who believes in evolution went to college this year, and I sent her a subscription of your magazine, *Creation*. She wrote to thank me for sending it to her, and I'll quote what she said about it. "This magazine is really good for me, because I spend so much time just looking at one side of the creation/evolution issue. It's nice to see well-thought-out scientific explanations."

Also, I bought some books from you this summer to take on my missions trip to Russia. I passed some out to kids at a non-Christian sports camp. They loved them! I gave the rest to a church to distribute themselves. There is such a need for Christian literature over there.

H.S., Iowa

Our family was very excited about receiving a personal reply from you recently. We now have another reason to look forward to receiving our *Creation* magazine. My oldest son is in college and he has had many opportunities to share his faith firsthand with his college professors. I hope you will be encouraged that your efforts in bringing the truth out to the younger generation bears much fruit. When you open the eyes of a young person, they never shut again. They develop an appetite for the truth and the growing process continues on. . . . Even though my sons and I have been very interested in studying creation science (my youngest even keeps his copy of *The Genesis Record* in the bathroom), my husband up until recently showed no interest. He is a pilot who spends much of his time away from home in hotel rooms and long hours in the cockpit. He asked me for something to read out of boredom and one day I handed him your book, *The Lie: Evolution.* He has since read several books on creation vs. evolution. No more boring discussions in the cockpit. He gets the whole crew involved in the creation-evolution controversy, as he loves the challenge.

I only mention this incident because the creation vs. evolution controversy affects every member of the family and society, not just our children. I think Christian parents fail to realize how important it is for parents and older members of the family to hold strong convictions and knowledge of creation that can be passed on to others whenever and wherever possible.

I've sent this letter in hopes that it is an encouragement to you and to the many others who struggle on the battleground of man's word vs. God's truth.

N.K., Michigan

All I can say is your magazine is fantastic! A friend of mine was having a terrible time in college biology with their slant on things, so I mailed him all my back copies of *Creation* magazine. The ammunition was greatly appreciated. I hated losing all my old copies, but they went for a good cause. So I don't have to lose any more copies, I am sending him his own subscription.

E.P., Texas

I am currently teaching a church school class of adults on creation, evolution, and Noah's flood using many materials which I obtained from AiG. I enthusiastically endorse *Creation* magazine and the *Technical Journal.* My number one goal is to re-affirm in my students' minds the accuracy and inerrancy of the Scriptures, including the first three chapters of Genesis. Of course, I am also giving them some ammunition to support a creationist world view. Thank you for your great ministry and your wonderful publications.

G.T., Oklahoma

I have thoroughly enjoyed your *Creation* magazine. Being a science teacher and enthusiast, I have lamented over my faith and the so-called "evidence" that science touts in every science publication. Now the truth is creeping out, and I am thankful to God for you.

I have several years of *Discover, National Geographic, Ranger Rick,* and *Natural History* magazines in my 7th and 8th grade classroom library. These magazines far outnumber my 8 or 9 issues of *Creation* magazine, which I display with pride. The interesting thing is my *Creation* issues are pored over every day. My other periodicals are collecting dust! The questions they ask most are answered in *Creation.* Thanks, again.

I recently went to my first AiG seminar. WOW! I was so impressed with the materials and the speakers. Ken Ham was entertaining and his views on how our beliefs in origins determine society were a revelation. I am determined to do what I can to further creation technology and education in my community. Buddy Davis's song, "Billions of Dead Things," still rattles through my head, and the other doctor who spoke on space has really given me "brain candy" to chew on.

I pray for you frequently and now believe that your information is the most important information I can share with Christians and non-Christians alike. Thank you, again, AiG.

P.S. Could you send me information on your new Creation Club idea. I would like to start one or sponsor it here at my school.

M.D., Junior High Science Teacher

We at Butner Prison Camp want to send our warm thanks for your love to prisoners here. We are babies in Christ Jesus, but thanks to your love offering, we can grow up in the Lord Jesus Christ. Thank you for the videos, cassettes, and books. We are grateful, brother. Thank you.

Inmates at Butner Prison Camp,
North Carolina

Praise the Lord! His love revealed in Christ is the best gift. Your kind and grace-filled letter really blessed my heart unto joy. It is my passionate desire to give a reasonable answer for the hope that we have in Christ, and your ministry has been so helpful. Your stand upon the Bible is cool and it honors Jesus. My ardent interest is any material that addresses the premises underlying creation vs. evolution and the authenticity and reliability of the Bible.

I deeply thank you and your ministry team for your kindnesses to me and the many you help as unto the Lord.

A.L., Illinois (prisoner)

Bless you! Your letter of July 24th was received with much shouting and rejoicing (mine)! Your generosity in providing the materials which you have outlined is a blessing indeed. When you and the AiG staff read that there is revival in the prisons, you can smile, knowing that you are a part of this move of God in our land.

J.W., Prison Chaplain, Florida

Thank you so very much for the literature you sent to me. It arrived so timely, as it appeared on the worst day that I have had in the 13 years I've been in prison. So bad was the day that I even contemplated ending my own life. Terrible thoughts for any person, let alone a Christian. But it was a pleasant blessing to return from the license shop to receive this "bundle of love" from AiG.

I have already loaned out the attractive *Creation* magazine after scanning it myself, but the interest in it by others has "wowed" them. Right now, I am happier with the answer to prayer that you've been to me, rather than the gifts themselves. A fellow in my shop asked me today, "Is there any light at the end of the tunnel for you?" I wasn't sure what he meant or why he asked me that, but in spite of the appearance, I answered that I am saved and Jesus Christ is the light.

Thank you, again, so very much for those who help and pray for your ministries.

N.F., prisoner in Wisconsin

Thank you sincerely for your obedience to our Lord and Savior for the blessings you have bestowed upon us here at the William F. Key Correctional Center. The men here are truly blessed from the availability and knowledge that the library provides, and we can see the changes that the Lord has made in so many lives. I pray that the Lord continues to bless you as much as He is blessing us. Once again, we would like to extend a heartfelt thank you for all that you have done for the edification of the kingdom of God.

S.B., prisoner in Oklahoma

I am a prison chaplain and God is doing a mighty work here. I thank God for the vision He has given us for the men here, most of whom are lost. The Christians here all need to grow in the grace and knowledge of the Lord. Your generosity reaches out to these men. It is impossible to know the value of your gifts to this ministry in this life, but one day, we'll see the results of your great effort in heaven! Keep us in your prayers.

G.H., prison chaplain, Florida

I have been writing to all of my friends and family about the creation message. I have sent out all of the tracts that you gave me in letters. My family and friends are beginning to rethink their position on creation. One friend told me that he didn't think that this topic was very important until I shared with him the ways that evolution was damaging our society. Last month a prime-time program showed that over 90% of the males in the animal kingdom are unfaithful to their mates. Then, they ask, should we really hold man to a higher standard than what his animal relatives are able to achieve? This is complete madness!

Now that my eyes have been opened, I can see the vast damage that evolution has done to all Christians. It is a faith-robbing evil. Let me tell you, I know evil. As inmates, we are taught that we must learn and control our animal instincts and not to take responsibility for our actions. Is it no wonder why most inmates return to prison.

Thank you for the chance to share with you how the creation message is working in my life.

D.F., prisoner in Pennsylvania

The creation seminar with Ken Ham directly impacted and changed my life.

I am a head teacher at a small day-care center. One of my favorite topics was dinosaurs. Little did I know it, but what I had gathered from research in various books and resources was a purely evolutionary view. Here I was a Christian and I knew so little about creation yet I was sucked into teaching children something I did not believe in myself. Ken Ham's seminars taught me just how little I really knew about creation and just how little faith I really had in the fact that God could create the world in six days. As a result of the seminar, I made a commitment to know God's Word and to study it in an unbiased way. I will now look only to God and what His Word tells me, rather than to make human presumptions about what He can and cannot do. I also realized that God longs to speak to us through His creation — we need only open our eyes to see that He really does communicate with us in this way. I was amazed to see how blinded I was and how accepting I had been of philosophies that were not godly, biblical, or proven in any way. I have also committed to teaching children only what I know to be true from God's Word and not just what I've learned from the world's perspective.

T.G., seminar attendee in New York

My husband and I are so thankful for your resources and bulletins on creation and the stand you take on God's Word. My husband takes your magazines to work, often sparking a conversation with a co-worker. They are a great witnessing tool.

C.G., Minnesota

I had the recent delight of attending your seminar in Birmingham. It was a great pleasure to hear you "live," so to speak. It has now been a year since I first heard a tape of yours, and wow, what a difference it has made to my Christian life. Now that I understand Genesis and see why it is so foundational to Christianity, my whole walk with the Lord has been empowered and strengthened. No longer do I feel unable to defend certain aspects of my faith. I used to be a defensive Christian, now I have become offensive (in a manner of speaking)!

I was especially challenged by what you said concerning Christian parenting. It is, indeed, their responsibility to ensure that what they have learned is from the Word of God (not man's ideas) before passing it on to their children. I would be grateful if you could share more of your thoughts on this subject with me.

R.G., United Kingdom

Ken Ham's cassette many years ago helped work through many tough questions. Since then I have given public lectures in Spanish and Arabic, giving evidence in the Scriptures against evolution.

M.H., Kentucky

About two or three years ago I wrote you and thanked you for publishing *Creation* because after reading some issues, my "atheist" husband finally let me and our sons go to church and even went with us a few times! Praise God! Through all these years and godly prayers of the faithful, God has brought him out of the depths of the world into God's saved family!

D.G., Oregon

One day Rainald (a physicist from Germany staying at our home) had an accident and was bedridden. I gave him the creation science tapes to listen to which converted him from an evolutionist to a creationist. That was the start of Rainald being saved. The story is going on and on. His girlfriend, later on his wife, was also saved. They together preach the gospel to anyone who comes under their roof. They are very hospitable people. One day we will see what the Holy Spirit did through a few tapes which were available just at the right time. Praise the Lord for creation science. Hallelujah!

C.H., Queensland, Australia

I personally was led to the Lord a number of years ago now via a creation science publication. . . . My husband has also since become a Christian, something I feel that the logic and sensible reasoning provided by the field of creation science has greatly aided.

S.W., Western Australia

Thank you very much for your efforts to reach the lost people in the world. Even though I grew up in a Christian home, I, too, was lost after graduating from a humanistic university and trying to live in the world on my own. Answers in Genesis provided me . . . answers! There are answers to life's questions that make sense in a biblical world view.

These answers led me to re-dedicate my life to the Creator. Praise God! This is the first time I have written to express my gratitude. A few years after college a friend loaned me a copy of *The Genesis Solution* video sometime in 1995. Since then, I have been utilizing your materials everywhere I go. I have an opportunity to teach English at a university in Russia. I plan to take several AiG books along to share with students and teachers. Please pray that I can be an effective witness for Christ.

W.H., Kansas

About a month ago, I gave a subscription of *Creation* to a co-worker. He was very impressed with the magazine, and it was an answer to prayer to hear him change his views from atheistic evolutionary dogma to truth from the Bible. A few short weeks after he got the subscription, we had a Bible study on his need for salvation. He believed that the Bible was God's valid Word and received Jesus Christ as his personal Savior. I know that God used your magazine to dispel error and deception from his mind so that he could clearly see and understand the Bible.

J.B., Kansas

I have used your material for several years, and have used them to bring three people to the Lord. Keep up the good work.

K.S., Victoria, Australia

Likewise, I say unto you, there is joy in the presence of the angels of God over one sinner that repenteth (Luke 15:10).

ENDNOTES

Chapter 7

1. David Barton, *Original Intent: The Courts, the Constitution, & Religion* (Aledo, TX: WallBuilder Press, 1997), p. 153. Quote attributed to Benjamin Rush, signer of the Declaration of Independence.

2. Benjamin Rush, *Essays, Literary, Moral and Philosophical* (Philadelphia, PA: Thomas and William Bradford Publishers, 1806), "Defense of the Use of the Bible in School," p. 210.

3. Ibid.

4. James Atkinson, ed., *Luther's Works, Vol. 44, The Christian in Society* (Philadelphia, PA: Fortress Press, 1966), "To the Christian Nobility of the German Nation Concerning the Reform of the Christian Estate," by Martin Luther (1520), p. 207.

5. Ibid.

Chapter 8

1. Donald E. Chittick, *The Controversy: Roots of the Creation/Evolution Conflict* (Eugene, OR: Creation Compass, 1984).

   Ken Ham, *The Lie: Evolution* (Green Forest, AR: Master Books, 1987).

   Kenneth A. Ham, and Paul S. Taylor, *The Genesis Solution* (Grand Rapids, MI: Baker Book House, 1988).

   Henry M. Morris, *Evolution and the Modern Christian* (Phillipsburg, NJ: Presbyterian and Reformed Publishing Co., 1967).

   Henry M. Morris, *The Long War Against God* (Grand Rapids, MI: Baker Book House, 1989).

   Gary Parker, *Creation Facts of Life* (Green Forest, AR: Master Books, 1994).

2. Jared Diamond, "Who Are the Jews?" *Natural History,* vol. 102, no. 11 (November 1993): p. 19.

3. Lewontin, Richard, "Billions & Billions of Demons," *The New York Review of Books* (January 9, 1997): p. 31.

4. Donald Kennedy, committee chairman, *Teaching About Evolution and the Nature of Science* (Washington, DC: National Academy of Sciences Press, 1998), chapter 5.

5. G. Richard Bozarth, "The Meaning of Evolution," *American Atheist* (September 20, 1979): p. 30.

6. Henry M. Morris, *King of Creation* (San Diego, CA: C.L.P. Publishers, 1980), p. 48.

   Morris, *The Long War Against God*, p. 304.

7. Ham, *The Lie: Evolution*.

8. Roy Wood Sellars (original rough draft), "A Humanist Manifesto," *The New Humanist* (May–June 1933): p. 58-61.

9. "Humanist Manifesto 2," *The Humanist* (September–October 1973).

10. John Dunphy, "A Religion for a New Age," *Humanist* (January–February 1983): p. 26.

11. AiG has compiled a collection of written statements from Christian leaders, schools, and seminaries that reflect their acceptance and teaching of an old-earth interpretation of Genesis. This list is on file at the AiG office in Hebron, Kentucky.

12. Pattle P.T. Pun, "A Theology of Progressive Creationism," *Perspectives on Science and Christian Faith — The Journal of the American Scientific Affiliation,* vol. 39, no. 1 (March 1987).

    It is apparent that the most straightforward understanding of the Genesis record, without regard to all of the hermeneutical considerations suggested by science, is that God created heaven and earth in six solar days, that man was created in the sixth day, that death and chaos entered the world after the fall of Adam and Eve, that all of the fossils were the result of the catastrophic universal deluge which spared only Noah's family and the animals therewith.

    Douglas F. Kelly, *Creation and Change* (Ross-shire, Great Britain: Christian Focus Publications, 1997).

    James Stambaugh, "The Days of Creation: A Semantic Approach," *C.E.N. Technical Journal,* vol. 5, no. 1 (1991): p. 70–78.

13. Personal letter on file at Answers in Genesis dated 4/13/96.

14. Chad Cray and Will Will, "Settling for Second Best: A Search for Truth," *The Crusader*, Northwest Nazarene College, Nampa, Idaho, May 20, 1998.

15. Ken Ham, "When Will the Church Wake Up?" *Creation,* vol. 17, no. 3 (June–August 1995): p. 16–18.

    Ken Ham, "The Necessity for Believing in Six Literal Days," *Creation,* vol. 18, no. 1 (December 1995–February 1996): p. 38–41.

    Ken Ham, "Fathers, Promises and Vegemite," *Creation,* vol. 19, no. 1 (December 1996–February 1997): p. 14–17.

Ken Ham, "Millions of Years and the 'Doctrine of Balaam,' " *Creation*, vol. 19, no. 3 (June–August 1997): p. 15–17.

Ken Ham, "Demolishing 'Straw Men,' " *Creation*, vol. 19, no. 4 (September–November 1997): p. 13–15.

Ken Ham, "A Young Earth — It's *Not* the Issue!" *Answers in Genesis Newsletter*, vol. 5, no. 1 (January 1998): p. 1–4.

16. Rev. J.A. Wylie, LLD, *The History of Protestantism*, Vol. 1 (N. Ireland: Mourne Missionary Trust, 1985 (first published in 1878), p. 303.

17. Ken Ham, *The Great Dinosaur Mystery Solved!* (Green Forest, AR: Master Books, 1998).

Chapter 9

1. Greg L. Bahnsen, *Always Ready* (Texarkana, AR: Covenant Media Foundation, 1996).

   Gordon H. Clark, *A Christian Philosophy of Education* (Jefferson, MD: The Trinity Foundation, 1988).

   Ken and Mally Ham, *D Is for Dinosaur* (Green Forest, AR: Master Books, 1991).

   Ken and Mally Ham, *A Is for Adam* (Green Forest, AR: Master Books, 1995).

   Ham, *The Lie: Evolution.*

   Ham and Taylor, *The Genesis Solution.*

   Henry M. Morris, *The Genesis Record* (Grand Rapids, MI: Baker Book House, 1976).

   Henry M. Morris, *Biblical Creationism* (Green Forest, AR: Master Books, 1993).

   G. Thomas Sharp, *Science According to Moses*, Vol. 1 (Noble, OK: The Foundation of a Biblical World View, Creation Truth Publications, Inc., 1992).

2. Duane T. Gish, *Evolution: the Fossils STILL say NO!* (El Cajon, CA: Institute for Creation Research, 1993).

   Ken Ham, *The New Answers Book* (Green Forest, AR: Master Books, 2006).

   Ham, *The Great Dinosaur Mystery Solved!*

   Henry M. Morris, *The Biblical Basis for Modern Science* (Grand Rapids, MI: Baker Book House, 1984).

Parker, *Creation Facts of Life*.

Gary E. Parker, *Life Before Birth* (Green Forest, AR: Master Books, 1992).

3. For example, the Creation Clubs program in public schools, initiated by *Answers in Genesis* in 1998. For more information, contact Kurt Streutker at: kstreutk@answersingenesis.org

4. Ham, *The Lie: Evolution*.

5. "The Top 100: Part 2," *The Barna Report*, Barna Research Group, Ltd., Oxnard, California, July/August 1997, p. 2. "Christian Lifestyle: 27% of born-again Christians have been divorced; 23% of non-Christians have been divorced."

6. Trevor McIlwain and Nancy Everson, *Firm Foundations: Creation to Christ*, Adult/Teenage Lesson Plans (Sanford, FL: New Tribes Mission, 1991), p. 3–15.

7. Ibid.

   Trevor McIlwain and Nancy Everson, *Firm Foundations: Creation to Christ*, Adult/Teenage Lesson Plans (Sanford, FL: New Tribes Mission, 1994).

   Trevor McIlwain and Nancy Everson, *Firm Foundations: Creation to Christ*, Children's Teacher, Vol.1–5 (Sanford, FL: New Tribes Mission, 1993).

   Trevor McIlwain and Nancy Everson, *Firm Foundations: Creation to Christ*: Children's Workbook (Sanford, FL: New Tribes Mission, 1995).

8. New Tribes Mission, *Now We See Clearly* (video), New Tribes Mission, Sanford, Florida, 1992.

   New Tribes Mission, *When Things Seem Impossible* (video), New Tribes Mission, Sanford, Florida, 1994.

9. Don Richardson, *Eternity in Their Hearts* (Ventura, CA: Regal Books, 1981).

10. Ibid. p. 129. It is not certain whether Richardson has made the connection as to why unreached tribes usually have stories of a Creator God or "sky-god." He seems to attribute it all to supernatural preparation of these peoples' hearts. While this may, of course, have happened, the fact that many also have stories of the flood, Babel, etc., strongly suggests that their cultural memory of the one true God is because of the truth of the Bible's real history of the world. All of us have a connection through Babel (Genesis chapter 11), and not so long ago (less than 4,500 years ago).

Chapter 10

1. Ham, *The New Answers Book*.
2. David Menton, "Inherit the Wind: An Historical Analysis," *Creation*, vol. 19, no. 1 (December–February 1996–97): p. 35–38.

    The World's Most Famous Court Trial (Dayton, TN: Bryan College, 1990).
3. Ken Ham, "The Wrong Way Round," *Creation*, vol. 18, no. 3 (June–August 1996): p. 38–41.

    Ken Ham, *Challenge to the Church*, audio cassette tape, 1997, Answers in Genesis, Hebron, Kentucky.

    Ken Ham, *The Monkey Trial*, video, 1997, Answers in Genesis, Hebron, Kentucky.
4. Ann Gibbons, "Mitochondrial Eve: Wounded, But Not Dead Yet," *Science*, vol. 257 (August 14, 1992): p. 873.

    Svante Pääbo, "The Y Chromosome and the Origin of All of Us (Men)," *Science*, vol. 268 (May 26, 1995): p. 1141–1142.
5. Steven A. Austin, ed., *Grand Canyon: Monument to Catastrophe* (Santee, CA: Institute for Creation Research, 1994).

    Steven A. Austin, George Van Burbach, John D. Morris, Andrew A. Snelling, and Kurt Wise, *Grand Canyon: Monument to the Flood*, (El Cajon, CA: Institute for Creation Research, 1995).
6. Ken Ham, "Millions of Years and the 'Doctrine of Balaam,' " *Creation*, vol. 19, no. 3 (June–August 1997): p. 15–17.
7. Ken Ham, "A Low View of Scripture," *Creation*, vol. 21, no. 1 (December–February 1998): p. 45–47.
8. Z@XrBearse (e-mail address), assistant to Bill McCartney, president and founder, Promise Keepers, personal letter dated October 1998, on file at AiG office.

Chapter 11

1. Morris, *The Genesis Record*.
2. Ham, "Millions of years and the 'Doctrine of Balaam,' " *Creation*, p. 15–17.
3. Weston W. Fields, *Unformed and Unfilled: A Critique of the Gap Theory* (Green Forest, AR: Master Books, 1976).

    Ken Ham, Andrew Snelling, and Carl Wieland, *The Answers Book* (Green Forest, AR: Master Books, 1996), p. 157–175.

4. Don Batten, "Some Questions for Theistic Evolutionists (and 'Progressive Creationists')," *Creation*, vol. 18, no. 3 (June–August 1996): p. 37.

Dean Davis, "Theistic Evolution: What Difference Does It Make?" *Creation*, vol. 20, no. 1 (December–February 1997): p. 48–49.

Werner Gitt, "10 Dangers of Theistic Evolution," *Creation*, vol. 17, no. 4 (September–November 1995): p. 49–51.

Ken Ham, "A Child May See the Folly of It," *Creation*, vol. 17, no. 2 (March–May 1995): p. 20–22.

Ham, "When Will the Church Wake Up?" *Creation*, p. 16–18.

Charles V. Taylor, "Biblical Problems for Theistic Evolution and Progressive Creation," *Creation*, vol. 17, no. 2 (March–May 1995): p. 46–48.

John Verderame, "Theistic Evolution: Future Shock?" *Creation*, vol. 20, no. 3 (June–August 1998): p. 18.

5. "Cosmic Breakthrough!" *Creation*, vol. 17, no. 1 (December–February 1994): p. 37–39.

Don Batten, "Physicists' God-Talk," *Creation*, vol. 17, no. 3 (June–August 1995): p. 15.

Ken Ham, "It's About Time Christians Take a Stand!" *Answers in Genesis Newsletter*, vol. 4, no. 1 (October 1997): p. 1–2.

Ken Ham, "What's Wrong with 'Progressive Creation'?" *Answers in Genesis Newsletter Special Insert* (October 1997): p. a–d.

Mark Van Bebber and Paul Taylor, *Creation and Time: A Report on the Progressive Creationist, Book by Hugh Ross* (Mesa, AZ: Eden Publications, 1995).

6. Ham, *The Lie: Evolution*.

Ham, "Millions of Years and the 'Doctrine of Balaam,'" *Creation*, p. 15–17.

Caryl Matrisciana and Roger Oakland, *The Evolution Conspiracy* (Eugene, OR: Harvest House Publishers, 1991).

7. Dr. E.O. Wilson, Harvard professor (sociobiology), *The Humanist* (September 1982): p. 40.

8. Craig Whitlock, "Gadfly's Crusade Is Winning Respect," *The News & Observer* (North Carolina), Sunday, January 11, 1998, p. 14A.

9. Ken Ham, *The Genesis Solution* video, (Gilbert, AZ: Films for Christ, 1987).

10. Ham, *The Lie: Evolution*.

11. Morris, *The Genesis Record.*

12. Ham, *The New Answers Book.*

13. Parker, *Creation: Facts of Life.*

14. Ham, *A Is for Adam.*

15. Ham, *D Is for Dinosaur.*

16. Ken Ham and Gary Parker, *Answers in Genesis* Video Series (including Study Guide), *Answers in Genesis*, Hebron, Kentucky, 1993.

17. Ham, *The Great Dinosaur Mystery Solved!*

18. Ham, Ken, "Where did Cain get his Wife?" *Answers in Genesis*, Hebron, Kentucky, 1997.

19. Ken Ham, "Dinosaurs and the Bible?" *Answers in Genesis*, Hebron, Kentucky, 1993.

    Ham, "Where Did Cain Get His Wife?" *Answers in Genesis.*

    Ken Ham, "Is There REALLY a God?" *Answers in Genesis*, Hebron, Kentucky, 1998.

20. Ken Ham, *Facts and Bias: Creation Versus Evolution — Two World Views in Conflict*, video, #9 from *Answers in Genesis* Video Series, *Answers in Genesis*, Hebron, Kentucky, 1993.

21. Carl Wieland, *Stones & Bones* (Green Forest, AR: Master Books, 1990).

22. Werner Gitt, *In the Beginning Was Information* (Bielefeld, Germany: Chistliche Literatur-Verbreitung e. V., 1997).

    Lee Spetner, *Not By Chance* (Brooklyn, NY: The Judaica Press, Inc., 1996).

Chapter 12

1. Pun, "A Theology of Progressive Creationism," *Perspectives on Science and Christian Faith — The Journal of the American Scientific Affiliation.*

Chapter 13

1. John Shelby Spong, *Here I Stand* (New York, NY: HarperCollins Publishers, 1999), p. 49.

2. Ibid.

3. *Arkansas Democrat-Gazette*, June 12, 2001.

4. United Methodist News Service, March 21, 2002.

5. Associated Press, January 26, 1998.

6. Hugh Hewitt, *Searching for God in America* (Dallas, TX: Word Publishing, 1996), p. 17–18.

ABOUT THE AUTHOR

Ken Ham is the executive director and co-founder of Answers in Genesis, a ministry dedicated to defending the Bible from the very first verse. Ken, a native Australian, receives hundreds of invitations to speak each year. He is the author of many books and articles on Genesis, and is the host of the daily radio program *Answers . . . with Ken Ham,* heard on hundreds of stations internationally.

Ken and his wife, Mally, have five children. They reside in the Cincinnati/Northern Kentucky area, where AiG has built a large creation museum and educational center.

FOR ANSWERS . . .

Too Many Questions
for Just One Book

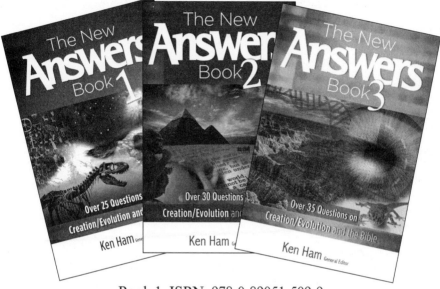

Book 1: ISBN: 978-0-89051-509-9
Book 2: ISBN: 978-0-89051-537-2
Book 3: ISBN: 978-0-89051-579-2

paperback • 384 pages • 6 x 9 • $14.99 each

Christians live in a culture with more questions than ever — questions that affect one's acceptance of the Bible as authoritative and trustworthy. Now discover easy-to-understand answers that teach core truths of the Christian faith and apply the biblical worldview to subjects like evolution, the fall of Lucifer, Noah and the Flood, the star of Bethlehem, dinosaurs, death and suffering, and much more.

Explore these and other topics, answered biblically and logically, from the world's largest apologetics ministry, Answers in Genesis.

Available at Christian bookstores nationwide

Join the
Conversation

Ask the experts

Build relationships

Share your thoughts

Download free resources

Creation
Conversations
.com

This is your invitation to our
online community of believers.

THE LIE:
EVOLUTION
by Ken Ham

Humorous and easy to read, this book powerfully equips Christians to defend the Book of Genesis and also opens eyes to the evil effects of evolution on today's society.

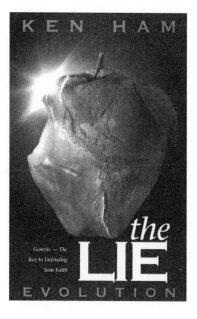

The Bible prophetically warns that in the last days false teachers will introduce destructive lies among the people. Their purpose is to bring God's truth into disrepute and to exploit believers by telling them made-up and imagined stories (see 2 Peter 2:1–3).

An eye-opening look at the harmful effects of evolutionary thought on modern culture and religion. Author Ken Ham uses his years of teaching and ministry experience to expose false teaching that is destroying children and families.

ISBN-13: 978-0-89051-158-9 • ISBN-10: 0-89051-158-6
paperback • 192 pages• $10.99

How Could a Loving God . . . ?

by Ken Ham

People assume Christians have all the answers — yet, in the face of tragedy, death, or suffering, everyone struggles to find just the right words to bring comfort or closure to those in need.

Sometimes, just hearing, "It is God's will" isn't enough. Sometimes just saying, "God will turn this to good" seems so meaningless when despair is so profound.

Often the pain goes too deep, the questions won't go away, and even the assurance of faith doesn't help. How could God let this happen? How can God love us, yet allow us to suffer in this way? What is the point of this — what is the purpose?

Ken Ham makes clear the answers found in the pages of Scripture — powerful, definitive, and in a way that helps our hearts to go beyond mere acceptance. When you grasp the reality of original sin — and all that it means — it creates a vital foundation for your heart to finally understand what follows.

ISBN-13: 978-0-89051-504-4 • ISBN-10: 0-89051-504-2
Paperback • 208 pages • $12.99

Available at Christian bookstores nationwide

If you enjoyed the book, please write a review at
Amazon.com, Christianbook.com,
and other online review sites.

Bringing You a Biblical Worldview

Connect with Ken Ham

 facebook.com/answersingenesis and facebook.com/aigkenham

twitter.com/aigkenham

blogs.answersingenesis.org

find out more about Ken Ham at: **answersingenesis.org**

Connect with Master Books®

facebook.com/masterbooks

twitter.com/masterbooks4u

youtube.com/nlpgvideo

nlpgblogs.com

find out more about Master Books at: **nlpg.com**